LETTERS

from

Mir

Also by Jerry Linenger

*Off the Planet: Surviving Five Perilous Months
Aboard the Space Station* Mir

LETTERS
from
Mir

An Astronaut's Letters to His Son

Jerry M. Linenger

McGraw-Hill

New York   Chicago   San Francisco   Lisbon   London
Madrid   Mexico City   Milan   New Delhi
San Juan   Seoul   Singapore   Sydney   Toronto

Library of Congress Cataloging-in-Publication Data

Linenger, Jerry M.
    Letters from mir : an astronaut's letters to his son / Jerry M.
    Linenger.
        p. cm.
    Includes index.
    ISBN 0-07-140009-5 (Hardcover : alk. paper)
    1. Linenger, Jerry M.—Correspondence. 2. Astronauts—United
States—Correspondence. 3. Mir (Space station) 4. Space flights.
I. Title.
TL789.85.L564 A4 2003
629.45'0092—dc21   2002009472

McGraw-Hill

A Division of The McGraw·Hill Companies

3 4 5 6 7 8 9 0   DOC/DOC   0 8 7 6 5 4

ISBN 0-07-140009-5

This book is printed on recycled, acid-free paper
containing a minimum of 50% recycled de-inked fiber.

To my children, John, Jeff, Henry, and Grace,
and to all of our children

May we never take them for granted

Contents

The collection of letters are presented chronologically and as originally written from space. Besides minor grammatical and spelling corrections, I sparingly modified some of the passages in order to provide context and to make the letters more understandable to the general reader. In no instance was the substance of a letter changed. Furthermore, this is the complete collection of the letters and not a sampling.

To be sure, the letters were never intended to be works of literature. They were in no way preconceived before my going into space. They are merely honest and sincere letters written from an astronaut-cosmonaut to his son while on a "business trip" orbiting the Earth. They were often written under severe time constraints and reviewed by tired eyes.

On the other hand, after reading the letters now that I have my feet back on the ground, I am satisfied that they were adequately written. They accurately reflect life in space as I lived it. The letters also expose the very normal human love of a father for his son. In addition to the substantive material, by carefully following the progression of the letters through time, the astute reader might detect subtle changes that were occurring in me. I assure you that the sense of isolation was profound and that the pressure-cooker environment on *Mir* was unrelenting. Such conditions do indeed change a person over time.

The first copy of this book will be placed on a shelf next to my son John's first photo album. In many of the photos from that particular album, his father is absent. That was my fault. But I plan on being seen as a part of many photos in his future albums, standing beside him and cheering him on.

Jerry M. Linenger
Suttons Bay, Michigan
July 2002

My original intention was to write some letters to my then fourteen-month-old son John so that later in his life he would know that his father was thinking about him while traveling in space for nearly five months.

My space mission did not go as planned. After a relatively calm first month on board the Russian space station *Mir*, a raging fire broke out and burned uncontrolled for fourteen minutes. Three-foot flames roared out of a solid-fueled oxygen generator. Choking smoke filled every nook and cranny of the station. The first respirator I donned failed. Desperate for air, I flung it off, and feeling my way along a bulkhead—the smoke was so dense that it was impossible to see—I was able to locate a second one by touch. Realizing that this was my last hope, I put the rubber mask over my head, threw the activation lever, and breathed in deeply and desperately. Oxygen flowed.

Once I recovered from near air starvation, I told myself, "We need to fight this fire, we need to get this fire out. We are trapped with nowhere to go. No mistakes, Jerry."

Amidst the smoke, the thought that I could die crossed my mind. I said aloud to no one: "Kathryn, I love you. Take care of John and our child to be. I will give it everything that I have to survive. I am sorry if I let you down." I was not at all certain that it would be humanly possible to overcome the odds against us.

Having beaten the odds, it was great to be able to continue writing to John. The experience of the fire probably helped me open up to him a bit more, to let my guard down. I realized that at any point in any of our lives, very abruptly, it could be all over. The fire was a stark reminder that life is precarious and that I was living on the edge, out on the frontier. "Why hold anything back from my son?" I thought to myself. "Tell him how much I love him. Try to convey to him what I consider important in life and what his father stands for. Try to tell him of the hopes and dreams that I have for him—before it is too late." My guard down, I began to write from the heart.

To be sure, the fire was only the beginning of the difficulties on board the aging Russian space station *Mir*. We then marched through a series of equipment failures that almost daily threatened the survival of the space station and, at times, our own survival. Losing computer control, we would tumble uncontrollably through space. Losing all electrical power, we would pass through the dark side of Earth in utter blackness aboard a "dead" space station. Losing effective cooling, we would work for weeks in ninety-degree-Fahrenheit heat. We worked constantly in an effort to keep the space station alive and afloat.

Living for a prolonged period of time literally off the planet and not merely "away" is the ultimate form of isolation. It was far beyond anything I had ever previously experienced, and I had experienced more than the average Earthling. The time I spent aboard aircraft carriers at sea and living on an island in the middle of the Indian Ocean was helpful in dealing with the isolation of living in space. But both these experiences paled in comparison to the degree of my being cut off from the world when in space. Two Russian cosmonauts and myself, looking

2

only at one another's stale faces and speaking only in Russian, together on cramped *Mir* for nearly five months. The isolation is profound. One feels very alone.

Not surprisingly, the experience changed me. The heavenly view of Earth in its entirety changed my perspective to one of a broader view of life. Step back and look at the big picture; step back and realize what is important in life. I learned to not take anything for granted, including the very air that I was breathing. I was transformed into a nearly fearless being, confident that if it were humanly possible to survive a given circumstance, I would survive. I would not panic; my heart would not race. Instead, I would calmly evaluate the situation and react to the emergency as I was trained to do. On the other hand, I realized that circumstances could be of such nature that no matter what my action, survival might not be possible. I learned to accept that terrible proposition.

At the end of the day, I would float over to a laptop computer and start talking with my boy through the writing of letters. Sometimes I would find myself uplifted by my reminiscences of him; other times I would find tears welling up in my eyes from missing him. The letter writing became a therapy of sorts for me, a time to reflect on the day's events and unwind by talking with my son. Letter complete, usually around midnight, I would fly over to the wall that I slept on and fall asleep.

Since I had so little free time, the letters to John were my primary means of personal communication back to the planet. My wife shared them with friends and family, all of whom were quite concerned over my well-being aboard *Mir*. Selected letters were also displayed during the flight on a NASA Web site on the Internet. I volunteered to allow them to be viewed by strangers around the world because I realized that I was privileged to be representing all of the people of the planet in space. By allowing them to share in the letters, I thought that people might be able to live part of my adventure vicariously. Upon the request of National Public Radio, I read four of the letters to John live over the *Mir* radio for use on the show *All Things Considered*. I had a hard time getting through that particular reading without becoming choked up. I was thankful that I was talking over the radio and not being seen on television.

After returning to the planet I began looking through the collection of letters that my wife had placed in a book for our son John. While unique in setting and experience, I realized that they were nothing special. Instead, the letters home expressed thoughts that most any father might feel for his children. On the other hand, how many of us never express those feelings to the children that we love the most? Perhaps the isolation or the constant danger broke down my own barriers to expression and allowed me to say the things that I should have been saying all along.

I am now willing to share the letters in their entirety with a wider audience because I think that they touch upon some human qualities and feelings that we all share. My hope is that the letters might excite within us the courage to break down our own individual barriers and to say what should be said to our children. Living off the planet and looking down on Earth as a whole made me realize that we all regard our families in much the same way. Letting our children know that we have unlimited love for them can only be a good thing.

My First Twenty Days in Space

The last glimpse that I had of my then fourteen-month-old son John before my five-month mission in space was through the rear window of our family car. It was the first week of January 1997 in Houston. He was sitting in his car seat; I was standing outside in the rain. I was waving to him; he was reaching for me. He wore a look of confusion when he realized that his daddy would not open the car door, release him from the confinement of his seat, and hold him.

I wanted to do just that—hold him—but could not. I was in medical quarantine. Launch was less than a week away. The medical staff at NASA viewed my son not as a beautiful baby boy, but rather as a reservoir filled with bacteria and viruses that were just waiting for the opportunity to infect another person. I was restricted from coming into direct physical contact with such a "contaminated person." The best that I could do was to watch him through the closed window.

He was beautiful. Big blue eyes with eyelashes so long that they need not grow another centimeter his entire life to remain functional. Blonde hair. Solidly built for a baby. Best of all, he was as feisty and adventurous as they come. He reminded me of myself.

5

When my wife drove away, I could see him turning, craning his neck as best he could in order to look at me. Moving his hand opened and closed, he waved good-bye. My heart sank. I stood alone in the rain for a good bit, until I was able to regain my composure. Eyes now dry but the rest of me dripping wet, I walked back into crew quarters and joined my shuttle crewmates.

The space shuttle *Atlantis* crew left the Johnson Space Center in Houston and flew to the Kennedy Space Center in Florida three days before launch. Our liftoff was on time, at night, and spectacular by all accounts. Two miles distant, John was cuddled in my wife's arms. Despite the four-in-the-morning hour, his eyes were wide open as he witnessed his first blastoff. The thunderous roar, the blinding light, and the raw power of the 7 million pounds of thrust shaking the ground and lighting the darkness did not bother him in the least. Like others who witnessed the launch, he followed the fireball with his eyes as the shuttle rose, rose, and rose still higher. Minutes later, as the cheering crowd became less boisterous and more reflective, and as the space shuttle *Atlantis*—already hundreds of miles downrange—could be seen only as a small object burning among the stars, he lost interest.

Inside the shuttle, the ride was violent and severe—akin to sitting atop an exploding volcano. After docking to the Russian space station *Mir*, we began transferring vital equipment, experiments, water, and food to the space station. I was the last "transfer item." Remaining on board *Mir* with the two Russian cosmonauts whom I had joined as part of the space station crew, I watched as the *Atlantis* undocked. The huge spacecraft then flew magnificently, rock-steady away from us until it disappeared from view, lost among the stars, on the dark side of Earth.

I unpacked my gear and began my work. The first few weeks aboard a space station are not unlike that of being in a new home after a move—boxes need to be emptied and storage areas organized. In short, one must become acquainted with the environment and settle into a routine. In addition, my body had to adjust from being an Earthling to becoming a spaceman. From walking to floating and flying; from eating with a fork to sucking food from tubes, from sleeping in a bed to sleeping inverted on a wall.

Connecting my space-hardened IBM Thinkpad computer to an electronic box that in turn was connected to the *Mir* telemetry system, I was able to send down data files as I completed experiments. In mid-January, I appended the first letter to my son John to the tail end of a huge experiment data file. Down below—in Mission Control, Moscow—the American contingent pealed off the minuscule Word file from the huge database file and emailed the letter to my wife and son, who were living in Star City, Russia. John received his first letter written from space on January 23, 1997.

Goodbye, Dear

Kathryn,

I just want to let you know how much I love you.

Remember how I sing to John when I am giving him a bath? "Your name is Johnchik . . . Johnchik . . . and you're the best boy in the whole wide world!" Well, you are the best wife and mother in the whole wide world.

I have a lot on my mind. Procedures. What I need to do in an emergency. And pondering how life will be for five months on the space station. But the predominant, overwhelming feeling is one of excitement.

I just worked out at the gym near crew quarters. Since it was three in the morning, I had the entire gym to myself. I happened to catch a news report on *NBC Early Morning*. They had a short piece about how the Russians are having serious financial problems, and in order to keep their space program operating they are now dependent upon shuttle flights. They then showed a clip of me getting into my harness in the "white room" (probably taken during our dress rehearsal two weeks ago) and reported that I would be the new resident on the space station *Mir*. The reporters commented that the weather looks good and that NASA expects a "go for launch."

Upon hearing that report, I just started yelling. Yahoo! Of course I knew that the weather was predicted to be clear, but hearing it once again, and knowing *I am about to blast off*— well, I felt overwhelming emotion. Anyway, I feel very prepared and am very pumped up to go.

I almost had to call you! It was four in the morning, but I almost could not resist dialing you. This behavior would not be much different than John screaming for you when he is hungry at all hours of the night, would it?

Kath, I am so proud of you. I will miss you tremendously and I am quite certain that it will hit me even harder after the hatch to the *Mir* closes and the shuttle leaves me behind. Things will quiet down and you will not be next to me at night.

Take care of our son. And of our future child inside of you. And yourself.

Do not hesitate to ask for help from all of our friends and family here on the planet when you need it, and know that you are always in my thoughts.

All my love,
Jerry

23 January 1997

I Am Still an Earthling

Dear John,

I decided before this flight that I was going to be a good father and write to you every day. This is my first attempt at that.

I realize that you are only one year old, and although I exaggerate your talents like any proud father would, I don't think that you can quite read this yet. No problem. When you can, you will feel good knowing that your father loves you.

Space flight is a dangerous business. I used to be pretty cavalier about it. But just before this launch, I started questioning what I was about to do. You see, I have so, so much to lose now. You and your mother.

I always liked adventures. I remember exhausting the elementary school library of mystery books by someone I think was named Orton. Trying to figure out the ending before the ending. Anticipating. Observing the happenings and trying to predict the outcome. Reading about people who found themselves in unusual and challenging situations, and then seeing how they responded.

Anyway, that curiosity characteristic is what got me on this space station. Oh sure, I went to lots of schools and did pretty well in our great U.S. Navy. In order to become an astronaut, I went through all the mechanics of the application and interview process. But the basic trait of insatiable curiosity is what drove me through all of that.

Space is a frontier. And I am out here exploring. For five months! What a privilege!

But, I sure do miss you. I want most of all to see you come stumbling around the corner, bellow out your big laugh when I give my "surprised to see you" look, and then watch you stumble back out of the room to repeat the same to Mommy in the other room. You are the best son in the world, John.

You know, although I am up here floating above Earth, I am still an Earthling. I feel the pain of separation, the pride of a father, and the loneliness of a husband away from his wife like an Earthling. And maybe even a bit more acutely.

Good night, my son. I'll be watching over you.

Dad

Propulsion and Suction

Dear John,

I now understand why I can take you out of your car seat and you stay sound asleep. Your life must be a huge struggle!

To be sure, I have reverted back to my childhood up here. I have to relearn how to clean myself, how to brush my teeth, how to eat without making a mess, and yes, even how to use a toilet. And by the end of the day my eyes can barely stay open.

Everything floats up here. And I do mean *everything*. Propulsion and suction are the keys to accomplishing the daily tasks of living.

For example, I can brush my teeth pretty well as long as I keep my mouth closed. If I open my mouth and breathe out just a bit, the toothpaste foam starts to float away. I keep a small two-by-two gauze pad nearby and carefully capture the stuff in it. Then, I transfer the dampened gauze to a plastic Ziplock bag, remembering to seal it tightly.

Eating can be fun. I think that I closely resemble you in my eating habits: constantly playing with my food. I can gulp peanuts as a fish would. The peanuts float; I open my mouth and pull 'em in! I guess that God made us all-purpose beings because once the food goes down the pipe, it stays down. Peristalsis. Who would have thought of it!

Love you, John. Good night my good boy.

Dad

PS: I almost forgot to tell you how I sleep. Strapped to a wall with bungee cords. I sleep like this in order to mimic the Earth sensation of feeling some pressure on my body, as if lying in a bed. And the best part of all, I sleep inverted, standing on my head, upside down. No, John, I am quite sure that Mommy won't let you try this!

26 January 1997
Letter A

No Bounds

Good morning, John!

I hope that you had a good night's sleep, because when you have a good sleep, Mommy has a good sleep, too. And she needs the rest, I'm sure. Being a "single parent" is tough business.

I hope that you realize what a great Mommy you have. It is not easy being married to a person that literally leaves the planet for five months.

Now that you have been in our lives for a year, we have learned that the love of one's own child is a special love. This love has no bounds and comes with no strings attached. Whether at two in the morning with a dirty diaper at hand, or nine at night feeling the warmth and serenity of watching you neatly tucked into your crib sleeping, we love you. You are a part of us, with Mommy's blue eyes and maybe a bit of my exploring trait. You open every cabinet in sight, probe every button that you can reach, and woof at every dog that you see during your outdoor walks. Our little boy.

Having said that, I have to go. It is time to work out on the treadmill once again. Running strapped down to the treadmill is a part of my continuing daily battle to keep my muscles and skeleton strong and Earth-hardened, so that I can walk once again with you when I finally get back home.

Love you, John. Pass along my love to Mommy.

Dad

Just a Normal American

Dear John Bartmann Linenger,

You have such a big name for a fourteen-month-old! Bartmann was Mommy's maiden name. I sort of wanted to name you Bart—close to her family name and after the mischievous cartoon character Bart Simpson. Bart is a young boy who is always getting into trouble. I like him. A boy should be adventurous, should push the limits a bit, and should not be afraid to try new things. Tom Sawyer was an okay kid. Anyway, I was vetoed and sounder minds prevailed.

I still feel like a boy myself. Space is one fantastic adventure. We are pushing the limits; we are on the frontier. Pioneering and living close to the edge. And I am privileged to be up here representing our country. I feel that strongly.

I have made it through launch. Seven million pounds of thrust. Docking. Two huge spacecraft coming together at

17,500 miles per hour. Undocking. A good-bye to my American crewmates aboard the most sophisticated spaceship to ever fly—the U.S. space shuttle. And now the task of keeping the life support systems running for the next five months on the *Mir* space station in order to survive. One great adventure, but an inherently dangerous one.

So, I want to pass down to you some information on your roots. Shoot, every parent should write this stuff down for his or her kids—life can take unexpected turns and be shorter than planned. I will just cover my half; Mommy will have to tell you her side of the story.

Your great-grandparents were the Pusavcs and Linengers. Great-Grandpa P. came to America from Slovenia. He was a shoemaker. And I mean that literally—he learned how to make shoes in Austria, then emigrated to America and set up a shoe shop in Chicago. I think they mistakenly dropped a few letters from his last name during his processing on Ellis Island, but, hey, he was just glad to be here. From New York, he hitched a train to Chicago, hobo style.

Your Great-Grandma P. is now ninety-two and as sharp as ever. You have already met her. Of course, she was Slovenian also. Chicago was famous for its ethnic neighborhoods in the 1920s. Capone never shot at either of them.

The Linengers came from Germany and settled near Detroit. Great-Grandpa Linenger was a building inspector and Great-Grandma Linenger a housewife with lots of kids who, for the most part, still live there in the Detroit area. Their kids had lots of kids, and this clan to a large extent accounted for the "great launch migration" to Florida. Over 1200 launch guests, a record for one astronaut, overwhelmed quiet Cocoa

Beach for my STS 81 shuttle launch. Seems that they were all so glad to see me gone (and I mean off the planet, gone!) for five months that they came down to celebrate.

Grandparents: You missed Grandpa. I miss my dad. He died in 1990. He was a telephone man and a great father. Best man I have ever known. I want to be like him for you, John. We will be playing "Catch" a lot and I will be at all of your games, all of your banquets, and all of your graduations.

Grandma L.: You remember her—she is the one who watched you every time that we returned to Houston for experiment training. Great Mom. Five children. Between her and Dad she managed to get all five of us through college. Your Uncle Kenny, barely.

Those are your roots, John. I will tell you more about myself in the next letter—but in general, I'm just a normal American. A very proud father and a man lucky to be married to your mother. I spent a lot of time going to school, based on my theory that if you listen enough, eventually something will sink in. I have twenty years of service in our U.S. Navy and now work in space. And I cannot wait for the arrival of your new brother or sister.

Be good, my son. I heard that you soon will be back in Star City, Russia. Dress warmly; I saw lots of white down there out the window of *Mir* today.

Love,
Dad

You Are the Highlight of My Career, John

Johnchek, Hooliganchek,

That's what we call you in Russia, you know.

Well, I promised that I would tell you about myself, so here goes.

I was a real ugly baby. Grandma says that when people would say, "Oh, let me see your baby," their next words were either "My," or "Oh my!" or they would simply stand there dumbfounded. I was glad to see that you took after Mommy.

We lived in a small blue-collar suburb outside of Detroit. One neighbor worked at Chevrolet. Another was a shoe salesman. Grandpa worked for the telephone company and drove a telephone truck—which was neat. Every once in a while he would sneak us kids into the truck, have us crouch down on the floor, and drive us somewhere. Mom drove Dad to work once or twice a week in order to keep the car for shopping. Then, all five kids would pile into the car at five o'clock sharp to go pick him up.

The public elementary school was right down the street. I walked every day. I was captain of the safety boys in sixth grade and I played Little League football and baseball. In junior high I played the same sports until I got knocked out cold in ninth grade making a tackle. After I spent one night "out of it" in the hospital, the light turned back on, and I ate ice cream. Unfortunately, I can't tell you about the ambulance ride because during that journey everything in my mind was all a big swirling tunnel leading toward nowhere. At the hospital, I must have overheard the doctors talking about drilling burr holes into my skull, because they said I snapped out of it just before the surgeons were about to wheel me into the operating room. After that incident, I switched sports to tennis and swimming and captained both teams. I don't recommend football for you, John.

Junior high was an adolescent whirl, better forgotten. High school went okay. Graduated right up there. Boring report cards.

Here is the true story as to why I went to the Naval Academy. I read a brochure about Annapolis that asked, "Are you good enough . . . blah, blah, blah . . . to become a midshipman?" I wanted to find out, so I sent in an application. I then took the entry tests and interviewed with my congressman—the whole schmear. Well, I got in. I was still trying to decide which school I actually wanted to go to when my dad read the part about no tuition at Annapolis. That settled that.

I did okay at the Naval Academy, but I did not have a lot of dates. Graduating, I went directly to medical school. I followed medical school by doing a surgical internship in San Diego (now, there's a pretty place), flight surgeon training in Pensacola (now, there's another pretty place), and, finally, duty with an aviation squadron in the Philippines (not bad either). This job entailed lots of flying to and from aircraft carriers. I returned to San Diego again, this time working as a medical adviser for an admiral, while at the same time doing some doctoring and some sports medicine research. I squeezed in some night school and regular school in between all of this. After I was selected to be an astronaut, Mommy and I moved to Houston. Two years later I was flying aboard the space shuttle *Discovery* for my first space flight (STS-64). Then you came along. And now I am living and working on space station *Mir*. You are the highlight of my career, John.

So John, that is your father. Pretty much your basic American, with the exception of being captain of the safety boys (that was special—I got to drink a cup of hot chocolate every winter day and I got to wear a badge). I really love our country and have always been proud to serve it. There is really no finer place in the world. You are one of the lucky ones because opportunities abound and you are free to choose. You can be anything that you want to be. No limits, no expectations.

I am sorry that I am not there right now to hold you and to teach you how to catch a ball. You did it once, but I think that the catch was a random event, kind of like when I lose a cable up here (everything floats) but an hour later it ends up right in front of my eyes. But I really believe that what I am doing will make a difference in your life and in the lives of all of your future classmates and friends. We will make up for lost time together when I get home, okay?

Tell your mother that I love her, that I am doing just fine up here, and that all the work we did preparing for this flight is paying off. And that I miss her, too.

Love,
Dad

27 January 1997

Some Tips from Your Dad

Dear John,

I just received a note from Mommy, who said that you have really been a great little boy lately. She says that you are at

18

the age where you try to mimic everything anyone does. And that you are laughing lots. And that everyone thinks you are so cute. Mommy agrees. Me, too. You are the best, John.

But the big news was that you had your first trip to the corner park. Mommy says that the rocking horse was your favorite, but you also did okay on your first swing ride.

All right, John. I can help you some on this. Here are some tips from your Dad.

1. Never get on a teeter-totter with someone bigger than you.
2. No matter how hard you try, you will never succeed at doing a loop-the-loop on the swing.
3. For additional speed down the slide: find an old waxed potato chip bag lying around (they are always blown against the fence nearby), sit on the bag, and then slide down. After going down the slide a few times, you will really be moving and all the girls will hold you in awe.

And talk about speed! Your Daddy was really flying today! I whizzed across the Isla de Chiloe, across the crest of the Andes (three or four of the taller peaks still snowcapped), across Patagonia, and out Golfo San Jorge in two minutes flat. Del Fuego in the distance. Clear. Spectacular.

Maybe someday you will be a geography nut like your father. For now, just make sure that you can find your way home from the park!

And John, pay serious attention to those books that Mommy always reads to you at night. Keep those eyes wide open, and do not go fading off halfway through the story like you usually do. If some day you go on a trip like the one that I am on, you will be trying to draw upon every bit of information, every bit of training, every morsel of practical stuff that you had ever learned in your whole life in order to succeed.

Now that I think about it, they do not make waxed potato chip bags anymore. Scratch that idea, John. Besides, perhaps it is better to start off slowly and to savor the ride all the way down.

Love you, John. Tell Mommy that Daddy sure was happy to get her note. And that I am just fine.

Dad

28 January 1997

We All Depend upon Each Other

Dear John,

Sleep while you can.

On *Mir* we are awakened every morning by the blast of the master alarm. And I mean blast. No nice, appropriately chosen wake-up music to greet the day with as on the shuttle. It reminds me of the difference between those old windup, loud-ticking, clanging alarm clocks and our modern clock radios that play very soft wake-up music. When the old-fashioned clock would start clanging, one would first have to make sure that one's heart was still beating before trying as quickly as possible to muffle the noisemaker under the pillow lest one's eardrum burst. The new clock radio alarms are so mellow that they allow one to snooze a bit more if desired and are easily ignored.

Regardless of the source of awakening noise, why is it that no matter when I go to bed I always want five more minutes of sleep in the morning? This phenomenon occurs no matter if I am sleeping in a bed on Earth or upside down on the wall in the space station. Maybe the sleep study that I am doing on myself can help people to find the answer to that profound question, along with the stated goal of determining how the quality and duration of rapid eye movement sleep is affected in space.

You know, John, there are thousands of unanswered questions, with many being much more important than why the morning alarm is always so darn unwelcome. The reason that I am up here is to attempt to answer some of those questions. A lot of scientists and other smart people down there on Earth have put together a great research program that I have the privilege of conducting. I try my best. The experiments are important, and I have to be careful to not make a mistake. Moving the wrong switch at the wrong time could totally ruin an experiment that may have been planned for years and was based on a scientist's lifetime of work.

I conduct the experiments in one of two laboratories. The laboratories are the space station modules *Priroda* and *Spektr*. These modules are thirteen-meter-long "tubes" that resemble the inside of a school bus. Each module comes equipped with power, telemetry, and computer hookups, in addition to an array of scientific equipment. Pretty impressive and complex stuff.

The lesson that I have learned from my work in the laboratory is that in order to do good scientific studies, many people must work together cooperatively. We all depend upon one another. The scientists depend upon me. I depend upon the NASA mission lead and his team in Mission Control–Moscow to schedule the work. And the folks in mission control depend upon the scientist for advice when things do not go as planned.

Together, we carry out the research protocols and, hopefully, we make life in the future a bit better for you. Anyway, that is the hope that keeps us going and striving to do our best.

Whoa. Perhaps I am getting a bit too serious for a fourteen-month-old. It boils down to this, John: Always try to do your best. When Mommy is changing your diaper, try not to do those wrestling roll reversals where you twist and turn and arch and do everything humanly possible to stay naked, your favored state of being. Try to sleep through the night. Try to smile and look at the camera for pictures. And try to understand why Daddy has to be away for a while.

Love you, my son.
Dad

29 January 1997

Don't Spit Your Toothpaste into Your Towel

Dear John,

An old friend just wrote. Said that he heard the floor creaking when he walked down his hallway and wonders if I miss things like that.

Although most fathers want their sons to be like them, I would rather that you not try to follow too closely in your Dad's footsteps. Along the lines of the famous "Do as I say, not as I do" phrase that parents always use, here is a list of "don'ts":

Don't try to fly from point A to point B just because you saw Dad do it.

Don't sleep on the wall.

Don't eat your food upside down above the table.

Don't spit your toothpaste into your towel.

Don't change clothes once every two weeks.

Don't eat your food directly from a can.

Don't go five months without a bath.

For now, Mommy is definitely a better role model.

Life is challenging, interesting, and productive every day up here. One fantastic collection of science projects, all located in the fantastic complex of the space station. The constant hum of generators, ventilators, and machinery is good substitute for creaking floors.

Good night, son. Sleep tight. I'll be watching over you as usual. Give Mommy a smile for me.

Dad

30 January 1997

You Would Enjoy Playing Hide and Seek Up Here

Dear John,

Let me tell you about my house.

Spectacular view. Unobstructed. Overlooking the oceans, the lakes, the rivers, the mountains. Plains and valleys. The city lights, the stars, and the other planets.

Six modules. One toilet. Dining area with two private sleep stations. Three-vessel garage: *Soyuz*, shuttle, and a

Progress supply-and-garbage truck. Each module a thirteen-meter-long tube.

Lots of extras. Two modules are new additions. They contain state-of-the-art freezers, computers, and gas analyzers. Built-in treadmills and bicycles for the recreational enthusiast. Low utility bills: completely solar-powered. Water from tanks, recycled urine, and purified condensate. Oxygen included. Radio, ham radio, and telemetry.

Maybe someday you will have a house like this, John. It is the frontier now, but perhaps perfectly normal by the time that you grow up.

I often try to picture you up here. At first a bit timid. Looking at me for some reassurance . . . then a little smile . . . then a big laugh. Skip the crawling and stumbling stage of life and just start *flying*!

For sure, you would enjoy playing hide and seek up here. Space station *Mir* is a maze with all kinds of nooks and crannies and hiding places behind panels. And you could hide on the floor, the walls, or the ceiling. And if you can hide like some of the missing cables "hide" around here, we may never find you!

You might not think so, but in space I still feel as if there is an up and a down. Although physically I feel just fine standing on my head or doing somersaults, I still prefer my feet toward the floor and my head toward the ceiling when working. Flying out of the intersection (the node), more often than not I end up in the next module upside down. Yet, I instinctively twist and turn until the lights are once again situated above me and the floor below me. Once oriented as such, I come in for a landing.

24

To enhance this feeling of Earth-normalcy, in each module the ceilings are white, the walls pale blue, and the floors an ugly orange-brown or a similarly ugly green. I am at this moment floating right side up, my computer attached to an all-Velcro table, and typing. If I do not think about my location and surroundings, I can lose myself totally and forget that I am in space!

I heard that you are heading back to Russia on Sunday. Try to be good on that long airplane ride, John. Crying once or twice is okay, since even we adults feel like crying after sitting still for eleven hours on a plane.

I will be looking for the contrail of your jet as you head across the ocean (usually, easily seen from space). And I'll be watching over you.

Love you, Johnchek, Hooliganchek.

Dad

31 January 1998

Someday, We Will Look Up Together

Dear John,

When I look out of the window up here, more often than not I see water. Since 70 percent of planet Earth is covered by ocean, that is the way the dice roll.

Attached to the ceiling I have a laptop computer that displays a map of the world. On the map is a trace of the space station's path over the planet. Every three days or so I enter into the computer our coordinates, using big long numbers like Z pos=1.8782342146. These coordinates correspond to our precise position in space at some exact time in the past. The computer then calculates where we must be at the present time. Kind of like those math problems you will someday hate: If a man leaves his house at 8 a.m. and travels at 60 miles per hour . . . blah, blah, blah . . . where will he be at noon?

Well, 17,500 miles per hour is very fast, and our position changes quickly. In order to plot a spacecraft's position over time, one must take into account drag and other factors such as gravity discontinuities that only rocket scientists know about. I am glad that the computer does all the work. After crunching the numbers, the computer spits out the *Mir's* present position and displays it as a moving dot superimposed over a map of the world.

If I see that we are approaching a landmass, I do my best to make it to a window. I go armed with an atlas and a camera. Points along the coastlines are the easiest to identify. For example, seeing Eighty-Mile Beach (western Australia) today was a piece of cake. Peaks, if snowcapped and standing alone, along with rivers—for example, the brown Amazon and its tributaries—are also easy targets. Cities are tougher to find, especially if located inland. Cities look like brownish denuded blotches in rectangular shapes. At night, the cities light up, especially in the United States, Europe, and Japan. Coastlines really light up. It is obvious from one quick glance out the window that most of the inhabitants of planet Earth live along the coasts. Obscuring clouds always make observation and positive identification of landmarks more challenging.

Today, I flew into sunset over Indonesia. I could see some huge, vertically developed tropical storm clouds whose tops cast three-hundred-mile long linear shadows across the (lower altitude) clouds below them and across the Earth itself. Then blackness. Then billions and billions of stars.

Like most people, I do not know the stars very well. And I would bet that a lot of people do not even take the time to look up at the night sky. Weeks, maybe even months pass, and we don't even look up.

John, when I get home we are going camping together—our first father-son camping trip. The Michigan woods would be great, but pitching a tent in the backyard would do. And we will look up together.

Miss you, John. Tell Mommy I love her.

Dad

Days Twenty through Fifty

Upon reaching the one-month mark in space, I felt totally adapted, totally at home. Floating seemed as normal as walking. Eating by sucking dehydrated food through straws came as naturally to me as using a knife and fork. I felt comfortable and at ease . . . as if I had lived my entire life in space. In short, *Mir* felt like home.

On February 23, the worst fire to ever occur on an orbiting spacecraft nearly destroyed the space station and the crew on board. We fought for our lives and won, barely. After nearly thirty-six hours without sleep, I finally collapsed on the wall that was my bed. I slept soundly.

Facing death only intensified my desire to talk to my son through letters. While I did not want to alarm my family down on Earth concerning the details of the fire, I did want them to know that I was okay. I also thought it imperative to let them know how important they were to me, how I thought about them in the midst of the fire, and how I drew upon the strength of my desire to see them again to rise to the occasion and put the fire out.

Stumped Mommy

Hello John,

Heard that you stumped Mommy yesterday. You saw and played with your first iguana over at astronaut Shannon Lucid's house. When you looked at Mommy with that questioning look of yours, she did not know how to make the iguana sound. I recommend that you stick with woof-woof; you do that one like a champ. And you will find a lot more occasions to use it than trying to imitate iguanas.

Mommy also said that astronaut John Blaha stopped by for a chat yesterday. Shannon and John are two fine people. They completely understand things up here on *Mir*, having lived it themselves. The next time you see either of them, say woof-woof for me, okay?

Friends are important. Without John Blaha showing me the ropes here on the space station during our five-day overlap, I would still be making wrong turns at the "intersection" node. All right, I will admit it: I still occasional end up in the wrong module, but I stick with my premise nonetheless!

Eat your food, John. None of that spit-out–the-mashed-up-green-beans stuff. Eating everything will pay off someday. Here is an example.

I have been working hard on some very complex experiments, rerouting power cables, and coming up with some new ways of organizing things on the station—in general, doing a pretty darn good job around here. Not a word from my Russian crewmates. But today, I ate buckwheat gruel for breakfast, the

Russian equivalent of Spam in a can for lunch, and *tvordik* ("sour cottage cheese"), beet soup, jellied fish, and currant juice for dinner, and were they ever impressed! First American they ever saw put down the whole packet of gruel, they said. And no one else even attempted the sour cottage cheese. I won them over. Mashed-up green beans would be welcomed.

Eat your food. Grow up to be strong, and brave, and true. Good night. Sleep tight. Don't let the bugs bite.

Dad

2 February 1997
Letter A

Or Is It Night?

Good morning, John,

Or is it night? Since you just flew halfway around the world from the United States to Russia, I'll bet your little body feels like it is daytime when, in fact, it is night. Biological clocks. Sunlight will soon reset yours; but up here things are different.

We keep passing from dark to light and light to dark every forty-five minutes. Although our watches are set to Moscow time, if I were to look out the window at noon, I would as likely see stars as sunlight.

This reminds me of when I was a surgical intern working long hours in the hospital. Sometimes I would walk out of the hospital expecting daylight, but would instead walk into the darkness of night.

The daily routine helps. The alarm goes off at eight each morning. We eat the normal three meals a day, but at rather odd times: 9:00 a.m., 2:00 p.m., and 8:00 p.m. Although I try to get to bed at eleven each night, more often than not, I attach myself to my sleeping wall at midnight. When I turn the lights off or slip on my eye covers, I attempt to trick my body into thinking that it is night, regardless of whether or not the sun is shining at that moment. Not much different than what submariners do.

Since we are talking of time, maybe now is a good time to talk of relativity. Einstein stuff. The continuum.

While I cannot claim to totally understand Einstein's theory, I have come to appreciate his genius. It hits me when I look out the window, trying to predict the relative motion of the stars. Or when I attempt to predict out of which window Earth will appear at a given time. These predictions can quickly become quite complicated.

The stars are basically fixed. In actuality, they move, but since they are so very far away, they appear stable in position. On the other hand, anyone who has become frustrated trying to see the constellations in the night sky knows that something has shifted. Over thousands of years, the position of the stars relative to each other has changed dramatically since the first person mapped out the picture of the crab, the scorpion, and all those other weird animals. Today, we need either new drawings or wild imaginations to see those figures outlined by the stars.

Getting more down to earth: Earth itself is spinning. Aboard *Mir*, we are flying in a ring around Earth. But since Earth continually spins underneath us, after each orbit we are over a different piece of real estate. Further complicating the picture is the fact that we generally want to keep the solar panels of *Mir* pointing perpendicular to the Sun. Solar panels are those big golden Sun-ray-catching panels that you see sticking out of *Mir*, which, incidentally, always seem to be getting in the way when we want to take photos! So we maintain an orientation whereby, relative to the Sun, those panels stay lined up. We use the term *Sun inertial position* for this, in order to baffle people and to sound like we know what we are doing. Keeping this Sun-pointing orientation means, however, that relative to Earth, the station is slowly changing which side is pointing down depending on which part of the orbit we are in. And to us, this means that a given window that previously was facing Earth may not be facing it twenty minutes henceforth.

Phew! Relative to something relative to something else. To be honest, instead of trying to figure it all out, I find it easier to float to various windows, glance out quickly, and see what I can see. Trial and error. As far as the motion of the stars, planets, and Moon go, I just *watch them* as they dance and sparkle across the sky. I can tell you that I once watched the Big Dipper rise over Earth low in the window, and set about twenty minutes later high in the same window. The view changes that quickly up here.

I think that Einstein must have had a differently shaped head. The hair flying out every which way proves that his electrical circuits were not standard issue!

John, since you were born with one half of my genes, I reckon that you, too, will be relegated into a life of trial and error, of muddling through. Let me tell you, in advance, that it is not as bad as it may sound. You will be able to enjoy the many surprises of life. For example, I just surprised myself by using the word "henceforth" a few paragraphs ago for the first time in my life!

Enjoy your day. (Or should I be saying, pleasant dreams?) I'll be watching over you and Mommy.

Love,
Dad

Been Sleeping Like a Puppy

Dear John,

Talked with Grandma L. and Unkie Ken today during an eight-minute communication pass. We were flying over China. The signal was originally picked up by a ground station antenna in Siberia, where it was then relayed to Mission Control–Moscow. Moscow then relayed my voice via satellite to the Johnson Space Center in Houston. Technicians there patched the signal via the U.S. phone lines to both my brother's home and my mother's home in Michigan in order that we might have a three-way chat. I could hear them. I was impressed. It is cold in Michigan.

Mom was concerned about my sleep. "Are you sleeping better?" she asked. A normal mother-type concern, along with the classics: "You look so skinny, eat more!" "Why don't you ever call?" and "You forgot to send a thank you to your third aunt, once removed, in China, for your birthday card." But in phrasing her question about my sleep, why did she use the word "*better*"?

I replied that I have been sleeping like a puppy the entire time since I arrived in space. (Based upon my experience with you, John, I have dropped the patently untrue phrase "sleeping like a baby" from my vocabulary.) I am, fortunately, one of the lucky few who feels no differently in space than on the ground. One hundred percent normal. She replied, "Well, that's not what I heard. I understood that you really had a rough time sleeping at first."

I will never fully understand where mothers get their information. Their knack for pulling information out of thin air is part of a running joke between my cousin Tom in San Diego and myself. A typical phone conversation between us might include the following dialogue: "Hey, Jerry, I heard from my mom who heard from your mom that you bought a new Saint Bernard that ran away yesterday and got hit by a Mack truck." The truth is that I have never owned a dog in my life. And during a phone conversation with my mom, I might hear her comment that she "heard Tommy quit his job and is getting married." If you knew Tom, the perennial bachelor, you would know that this is an impossibility; it would never happen.

But this tops all! I am in space and sleeping just fine. And although I have not heard visitors knocking on the door of *Mir* lately, she heard from *someone* that I was not sleeping so well. Brother Ken chimes in to the conversation: "Mom, it was me who said that I wasn't sleeping well." Ken's dry humor shining through. The mystery remains.

Anyway, my son, the lesson is this: Don't believe everything that you hear. Unless it is your papa talking. And know that your mother and father will always be thinking of you, worrying over you, and making sure that you get your rest. You can count on it.

Good night, little John.
Dad

Another Father-Son Talk

Dear John,

Mommy just sent me a note saying that you are so cute. Real smart, too. And that you have learned how to give a kiss. This combination can only spell trouble. We had better have another father-son talk.

I am no expert. No man is. Only women understand these things, but they leave us men in the dark. They refuse to explain a thing to us. That is why we just sit and watch football games on TV.

Be selective. Don't give a kiss on impulse. Sleep on it for a night, then if you still like the idea, well, okay.

Women in general know a lot more about important things in life than us men do. By important, I don't mean work or school. I mean how to get along with others, how to be considerate, how to live peacefully. Watch your mother. She is a great role model, John. Learn from her and you will be a fine young man some day. Kinder and gentler.

I cannot wait to receive my first peck from you. Maybe you can save one up for my landing day. And days thereafter. Then you can teach your future brother or sister all about it.

Speaking of which, Kathryn said all is well with her pregnancy. Doctor exams and tests are all A-okay. I am hoping for another boy. Not that I prefer boys to girls, but that I just prefer children. Let me explain.

I want at least four or five. If the next one is a girl, Mommy might be content with two. But another boy? I know she would try once more for a girl. (The trying part I will explain to you later; stick with kissing for a while.) And maybe even another time. And so on, and so forth, and so on. Pretty soon, we'll have our own Linenger baseball team!

There is plenty of land out there. I have seen the planet. It is amazing how we all clump together in our towns and cities. Look at Australia. Big-time empty. And majestic, with aqua-blue reefs surrounding the continent. Four or five more humans would fit in nicely on planet Earth. And should Earth become too crowded, there is plenty of room up here.

Okay, John. Now I can tell you to give Mommy a kiss good night for me. Do it, please. Love you both.

Dad

4 February 1997

Physicists Love This Stuff

Dear John,

I bet that you will be glad to get back into your own crib, play with your own toys, and see all of your Russian friends again. And they will, no doubt, be overjoyed to see you again.

They will see how you have grown, what new tricks you have learned, and how much smarter you have become. Have fun impressing them, John. When I return, I am sure going to have a blast enjoying your new self. There is nothing finer on planet Earth than your own son. All fathers must feel that same way for their sons. And I would suspect the same with daughters. Children are a real gift, a real joy.

An experiment surprised me today. Fluid physics. Wetting and surface tension. Measuring the reaction of fluids to varying wedge angles and examining liquid bridges. Physicists love this stuff! They are trying to predict how fluid reacts under differing conditions in weightlessness. Undoubtedly, the investigators will analyze the films of what I performed up here for hours. To each his or her own.

You would like the device I used to perform the experiment, John. It was like a toy. I opened a valve and squirted this red Kool-Aid-appearing liquid into a chamber. After turning a dial to raise the fluid level, I would then turn a different dial to change the "squeeze" angle. I would then go back and forth between the dials until the critical angle was reached—whereby the fluid was supposed to shoot up the wedged walls in a smooth motion. Operating this device was not much different than operating an Etch-a-Sketch.

The surprise was this. The scientist who designed this thing expected the fluid to fill the "floor" of the second chamber when I opened the valve. But the environment of space is different. Earthly assumptions often do not hold. To the fluid, the "wall" was just as good a place to start off as the "floor"—so it started filling there. The red fluid spread up the "wall" immediately, formed a meniscus eventually, and then made its way along the "floor" and "roof" when I decreased the squeeze angle.

If I lost you, let me simplify. Imagine an empty swimming pool. Turn on the hose to fill the basin. The pool begins to fill up, but not from the bottom up, but from one side across toward the other!

38

In my view, there could not have been a better result. Something unexpected happened. We advanced our knowledge of the fundamental behavior of fluids. And it was only possible to do this in space. The mold killed the bacteria.

Well, John, I am really tired from all my painstaking work on the Etch-a-Sketch. Time to crawl into my sleeping bag. Pleasant dreams to you and Mommy. I love you both.

Dad

Like Being in a Rowboat

Dear John,

I am heading toward the coast of Africa. When I arrive, I will try to snap a picture of where Mommy used to spend time doing volunteer work: Accra, Ghana. Lake Volta is an easy find from space, so by using its location as a landmark I should be able to locate the nearby city of Accra.

No joy. Clouds and falling light. Plus a brownish, dusty hue over the deserts of Africa.

Sasha is running on the treadmill, medium pace. I didn't see him go there. And it is not Valeri. Nope, it is definitely Sasha, and he is running on the treadmill in module *Kristall* and not on the treadmill in the module *base block*. I know who it is and what he is doing not by sight or sound, but by feel. I can feel him. Frequency about 1 hertz.

The computer and I are going up and down right now. It feels similar to being in a rowboat, near the shore, after a ski boat has gone past. A gentle, but definite swaying of the entire thirteen-meter tube in which I am presently located. The station is absorbing the force that Sasha imparts to the treadmill, and *Mir* sways, resonates. If he were to either slow down or speed up a bit, I would feel nothing. My peaceful float would return. I heard that when Shannon Lucid was on board she had to stop running at her natural pace because the station would resonate at a dangerous level.

You would be in heaven, John. The motion would rock you right to sleep!

In order to avoid such disturbances from affecting some of our experiments, say, for example, growing delicate protein crystals (useful in designing more effective medicines), we mount the vibration-sensitive experiment on an isolation mount. This device basically uses magnetic fields to levitate a platform—the floater—on which I mount the experiment. The device acts to isolate any disturbances and keeps things nice and steady.

We also measure any disturbance nearby the experiment using accelerometers. And some folks are working on refining a device that goes to the source—the treadmill—in order to isolate it from the structure. I ran on a treadmill mounted to this device on my way up here while still aboard the shuttle. The isolation mount was too big to put on the floor, so we mounted it from floor to ceiling. We then attached a treadmill to it. Because of this arrangement, I felt as though I were running on the wall! Now *that* felt strange and looked even stranger to the other astronauts watching—with me running horizontally. In space, nothing is quite the same. There are new surprises every day.

If you are not exactly following the fine details of what I am talking about, that's okay. Heck, you are only one and almost a half years old. I have been studying how to run these experiments and others for over a year now. If you are fascinated, that is what is important. These specific problems will, undoubtedly, be solved by the time that you grow up. But if you have a healthy dose of curiosity in you, it will serve you well no matter what problems of the future might need solving.

Sorry that I talk so much about work, but it is what I do up here all day and half the night. The sense of accomplishment, the feeling that what I am doing might make a difference, is what keeps me going. But when I crawl into my sleeping bag at night, I always say a prayer for you and Mommy, always think of you—and then fall asleep content and with a little smile on my face.

Love,
Dad

6 February 1997

An Unforgiving Place

Dear John,

Wow, what a day! Busy, busy, busy. Almost as bad as when Mommy goes into Moscow to pick up groceries and I have the "duty," chasing you around the house. At least you clonk out for an hour or so, allowing me time to recover. Up here it is nonstop work. Writing to you is my one moment of peace.

The garbage truck left today. Called *Progress*, the spacecraft had arrived with all kinds of goodies. Letters from home, fresh food, and clean clothes being among the most important items from the crew's perspective. But *Progress* is mainly filled with fuel, water, and needed equipment to keep the space station running. The spacecraft comes up unmanned and docks automatically. All commands to the spacecraft are radioed up from the control center in Moscow.

An almost identical docking system is used on the Russian manned capsule, the *Soyuz*. A *Soyuz* brought up my two present Russian cosmonaut crewmates almost five months ago. In a week a different *Soyuz* will bring up their replacements— my future crewmates. I will be going home on the shuttle when it docks in late May.

Oh, back to the garbage truck. After unloading the *Progress* we begin to refill it, but this time with trash. Old broken equipment, toilet (waste) holding tanks, and dirty clothes. We then close the hatch and release the docking clamps, which in turn allow springs to push the spacecraft away from the space station. After flying freely for a day or two, and on command issued from the ground, the *Progress* fires its retrorockets and reenters the atmosphere, burning up and disintegrating. Burning up and disintegrating is exactly the fate that my two-week-old worn and smelly clothes deserve!

Today, I sat directly in front of the hatch from which the *Progress* departed. I could both feel and hear the springs pushing it away. When I looked out of a tiny window adjacent to the hatch, I could see three of the vessel's running lights moving away. The spacecraft was stable and slow-moving. I then saw the spacecraft thrusters firing, which put on a pretty neat light show.

Tomorrow we go for a ride. The three of us will first climb into our space suits and then into our *Soyuz* capsule. We will undock from a docking port located at the far end of the space station, drive over to where the garbage truck was parked previously, and dock at this new location. We will then verify that we have a good airtight seal between the space station and us. If that checks out, we will open a couple of doors and it will be "home, sweet, home" again.

The reason? We want the "fresh" *Soyuz*—the one that will be launching next week—to park in the place that the "old" *Soyuz* is presently located. Plus, the port that we will be docking to is pretty old (ten years or so), and it is best not to leave it open to the bombardment of space debris and particles.

Everything will be fine. But space is the frontier, an unforgiving place, and things could go awry.

For example, should we undock successfully but then be unable to redock, the only option would be to head home. There is a limited supply of oxygen and fuel on board a *Soyuz* capsule so we could not live in the capsule for long. If we are unable to redock and are forced to fly home to the planet, after a fiery reentry the capsule would come down under parachute and then plop down rather unceremoniously and with a final, firm bump in the middle of a desert in Kazakhstan. I would be without my passport. That might be the worst part of it!

You can sit here and imagine a lot of less-than-desirable scenarios. If a control thruster on our capsule fails to shut off, we could get ourselves into an uncontrollable spin. Or if the docking mechanism malfunctions and does not hold us tight enough together to get a good seal, we would be unable to open the doors. Anyone who has tried to fix a leaky faucet knows how difficult it is to get a watertight seal, one that is "not too tight and not too loose." Well, airtight is even tougher to achieve. A leak would mean that we would lose all of our breathing air to the vacuum of space should we open the hatch under such conditions.

Anyway, everything will be fine. Although we think about those "bad" possibilities in order to be prepared to react appropriately should they occur, the odds are that everything will go smoothly. And it will be another grand adventure for your daddy, John.

I hope that your adventures around the hall, through the kitchen, and into the living room—opening every drawer in sight, unhooking every reachable telephone, and banging every pot and pan—are as enjoyable.

Good night, my little adventurer. Give Mommy one of those little kisses of yours for me. Thanks.

Love you,
Dad

7 February 1997

An Afternoon Spin in a Spaceship

Dear John,

I just want you to know that I am back home safe and sound. We left at two in the afternoon from one door of the space station and came back in through a different door at around ten at night. Quite a day.

44

Here's what we did in a nutshell. Closed the *Mir* hatch and checked that it and a second hatch within the *Soyuz* spaceship were airtight. Fired some thrusters to check that they were working properly. Waited. Then we departed when we came into a zone-of-communication with Mission Control–Moscow.

Concerning the undocking, I felt it, heard it, and saw it.

I felt a smooth, yet firm, push-off, a springlike action. An ink pen floated forward inside the spaceship.

I heard the *Soyuz* thrusters firing. Not an explosive sound, but more like low growls. To the cadence of short and repetitious bursts.

As I looked out the porthole window located directly to my right, I could see Earth spinning below and flashes from the firing thrusters in the foreground. The space station docking port moved steadily away, until I could see module *Priroda* in its entirety out of my window. As we moved yet farther away, I could see the entire space station—all six cylinders—looking like giant Tinkertoys floating in space.

The whole time I was strapped into my seat and crouched within the confines of the tiny *Soyuz* capsule with my knees almost to my chest. Since I was wearing my bulky space suit, I could hear the sound of the space suit ventilator humming and feel cool air trickling over my sweaty body inside my airtight suit. The *Soyuz* control panel was literally in my face and included a navigationally useful spinning miniature globe enclosed in a glass case, a myriad of push-button switches, and caution and warning lights. Operation manuals, written in Cyrillic, were opened and floating. And finally, I once again felt the sensation that we were moving, going somewhere, flying.

Oddly, although when we're inside the space station we are indeed flying fast, it does not *feel* that we are flying fast or, for that matter, even moving. The speed is constant and unchanging, and only by looking out of the window does one sense that we are moving at all. But in the *Soyuz* spaceship, it felt like we were in an airplane or jet, sitting in the cockpit, *moving* and flying. In addition to the seat-of-the-pants feel of the changing acceleration, Earth below was moving, and the space station *Mir* changing relative position outside of the window. I could feel the gentle thrust.

During the physical docking, I felt and heard a thud, then felt that the spaceship was being yanked around a bit. I was glad to see that the pressure inside the *Soyuz* held, confirmed by both the gauge in front of me and the lack of any unusual popping sensation in my ears. It was a relief to open the door to the space station once again and to get out of the cramped and claustrophobic *Soyuz* capsule.

It felt like coming home after a vacation. At first, all of the lights were out inside the *Mir*. The station looked familiar, but somehow changed. Being back inside my "home" gave me a good, warm feeling inside.

The Russian tradition after arriving at the destination of a trip is to sit down and eat salt and bread together. There is a bread roll that resembles a plain hamburger bun among our food selections. We have nicknamed it San Antonio bread. A dry and tasteless bread, it makes Wonder bread taste flavorful in comparison. I unwrapped one of the rolls, broke the bread into thirds, and with an almost straight face said that eating San Antonio bread was an American tradition after going out for an afternoon spin in a spaceship.

So, John, that was Daddy's day. Hope that yours was as great as mine was.

Pleasant dreams, Johnchek.

Dad

Tougher Than Sitting in a Rocket Waiting for Launch

Dear John,

I wonder if you could pass this note to Mommy. Tell her to read it to you for your bedtime story. Sorry, there are no pictures of bears, no flaps to turn, and no slide-outs to pull. But Mommy's voice and closeness are what really count the most in bedtime stories anyway, right?

Kathryn, I love you. Feel that as strongly as ever. Very alone out here in space. When it gets quiet, I think of you for comfort. Sometimes, alone, I start laughing aloud thinking about something that we had done together or some phrase of yours. You are with me.

Memories like our wedding. Chicago. Me pacing in a room behind the altar with the altar girls and waiting. Dressed in my formal white uniform. Other Navy officers escorting the guests to their places. Waiting. The altar girls talking too much: "This is so cool! Wow, swords! Oh, she's beautiful!" I glance at my watch and notice that it is already ten minutes past the scheduled wedding start time. And I am really getting nervous. The

47

talkative altar girls—and I thought that people were supposed to be quiet in church—query me further: "Did you meet on a ship?" Twenty minutes late. "What are all of those ribbons on your uniform for?" Thirty. "This is so cool, really cool!"

I send my best man, my brother, on a mission to determine what is causing the delay. He returns to report that there is no problem with the bride, only with "lost somewhere in Chicago" bridesmaids. This gives me some relief, but my palms are sweaty nonetheless, and the altar girls continue to barrage me with questions. This waiting at the altar was tougher, by far, than sitting in a rocket waiting for launch.

The priest finally rescues me from the curious altar girls and leads me to a position in front of the altar. Ah, there you are. Gorgeous. White dress. Me standing there, waiting, but all eyes on you. I take a deep breath and tell myself, again, to try to relax. Your dad gives you a kiss good-bye and hands you off to me. I take your hand and feel comfort. I feel better together than alone.

And I still do to this very day, Kathryn.

John, if reading this letter does not suffice for a bedtime story, try coaxing Mommy into reading about green eggs and ham. And do not worry if you don't understand all this. You'll learn someday. Good night to you both.

Love you both very, very much.

Dad/Jerry

This letter to my wife was begun just before, and then finished directly following a rare communication pass where I was able to talk to and see my family via live video.

John Looks Bigger and Tougher

Dear Kathryn,

I can't wait to see your face! And maybe our son's, too!

Only half an hour until the live video family visit. Maybe this event is not a big deal to you, but I am excited! It is something that I have been looking forward to all week. If it works, seeing you will undoubtedly be the highlight of my week.

And Happy Valentine's Day. Love, love, love you! And Happy Birthday, too. I am wishing you these greetings now because you never can depend on the *Mir* communication system. You are the best wife in the world, dear.

I have seen so many neat-looking places out the window that I now want to visit. New Zealand, for instance. What do you think? The four of us!

Love you. I have got to go and talk!

Jerry

PS: I just saw you guys and you both look great! John looks bigger and tougher—just fantastic! And you, my dear, are more beautiful than ever! The whole time, I just wanted to reach out and grab you!

Be careful; remember that you are pregnant. Don't go traveling to some out-of-the-way place where finding a good doctor would be difficult. You have to think about our next little one, too (smile . . .).

J

Human Being Questions

Dear John,

I just finished talking to Grandma Linenger. During a CNN interview with John Holliman, they surprised me and had my mom on the telephone.

He and I talked briefly before the interview. He said that all mothers are alike. They all worry over their children. He related that when he was in Baghdad during the start of operation *Desert Storm*, he was under strict orders to call his mother every day to assure her that all was okay.

My mom just said that I am in her thoughts and prayers, and to take good care of myself. I told her that I am doing just fine and sent my love. Ten or twenty or forty years from now, I bet that Mommy will still be worrying over you, John. Very special and nice, a mother's love.

I think that a father's love is not much different. Rougher hewn, but just as strong and endless. And maybe less expressed, but present nonetheless.

I did a second interview afterward with *Discovery* Channel, Canada. I was briefed that they would probably be asking about a Canadian experiment called microgravity isolation mount. Since the *Discovery* Channel usually does some rather serious documentaries, I decided I had better brush up a bit. I memorized once again the fact that the device isolates in the frequency range of 0.01 to 100 hertz, that Queld, another Cana-

dian experiment that sits atop it, measures diffusion coefficients in metallic binary systems, glasses, and semiconductors.
You know, all that kind of stuff.

Sure enough, they asked about these experiments. My first
reply painted the big picture, with my saying something to the
effect that the mount isolates the experiment attached to it
from disturbances on the station, something that we call g-jit-
ter. I then showed them a bubble of orange-mango drink floating to demonstrate how unique the space environment is, and
how we can better study the fundamentals of fluids after
removing some of the Earth-gravity created confounding factors. He immediately moved to the next question—"How was
your ride in the *Soyuz* capsule?"—or something along those
lines. This was followed by "How do you feel?" and "What do
you see out the window?" Softball stuff. I could tell he did not
want to talk about the technical stuff anymore than I did. We
both relaxed and had a nice chat.

The bottom line is that most people just want to know
what it is like up here: How do you feel, physically and psy-
chologically? What do you do? What surprises you? How
does it feel to undock, to fly in a spaceship, to be isolated, to
live in a dangerous environment? How do you deal with it?
What does your wife think? What does your mother think?
Are you claustrophobic? Human being questions. I try to
answer honestly, unafraid to talk about the softer side of this
great adventure.

Today I saw huge dust storms originating in the Sahara
Desert of Africa. Lake Chad is drying up. Five minutes later,
the Nile River, the distinct triangle of the Sinai Peninsula, and
the Red Sea all came into view. Then Elbrus and the snow-cov-

ered Caucasus. One month and twelve million miles under my belt. Quite a trip.

Sleep tight. Don't let the bugs bite.

Dad

Getting Crowded Up Here

Dear John,

Space is getting crowded.

Yesterday, a *Soyuz* launched bringing up the two replacement cosmonauts to *Mir*, along with a short-stay German researcher. Today a shuttle launched, headed to do some routine maintenance work on the Hubble Space Telescope. That makes three (the present *Mir* crew) plus three (the *Mir* replacement crew) plus seven (aboard the shuttle) of us—thirteen human beings, all in space at the same time. Lucky that there is a lot of universe up here!

I wanted to remind you that Valentine's Day is coming up Friday. It is a day that all little boys dread. You have to sort through these little boxes of cards and try to find some that say something like, "I flip over you" with the picture of an acrobat, to give to the girls in your class. By default, the boys get all the ones splattered with hearts that say, "I want you to be my one and only Valentine." There are not a lot of good choices. You will see soon enough.

Since you are only a year old, this year it won't be so bad. Just give out some of those kisses that Mommy said that you learned to give and all the women will think that you are the best. You might even get some heart-shaped candies out of the deal, John. And give Mommy at least a few of those heart candies for me, and tell her that she is and will forever be my one and only.

Another reminder: Mommy's birthday is the following day. Double whammy. But better than Christmas Eve birthdays like the twins Unkie Kenny and Auntie Karen have had to endure. They always get something that was originally intended as a Christmas gift for their birthdays. And yes, we have all kinds of twin pairs on my side of the family, so maybe Mommy will surprise both of us come June with a new brother *and* sister for you. A real double whammy!

For Mommy's birthday, try to be an especially good boy. Let's see. Maybe just stay quiet in your crib all night long. Then sleep in until ten in the morning. Instead of wetting your diaper, try using the bathroom. No playing bongos on the pots and pans. No spitting out your food. Sit quietly and read a book. Have all your toys put away neatly. At naptime, give Mommy that "what a great idea, just what I wanted to do" look and lie down without whimper.

Ah, heck. On second thought, we both love you just the way you are. Be yourself. Kathryn will feel blessed; even if a bit worn out. You are the best gift in the whole wide world.

Just hum a "Happy Birthday to You," eat some cake, and have some fun with Mommy as always. Smile lots. Chase her around. Suck your thumb and pull your ear when you are ready for your bedtime story. And tell her that Daddy will be thinking of her on her special day.

Pleasant dreams, Johnchek. I hear you are getting bigger every day. I miss you.

Dad

A Heart-Shaped Photo

Dear John,

The newly arrived crew just brought me a letter from Mommy. And a fantastic photograph of you and her together. The photo is shaped like a heart for Valentine's.

Well, the photo is now hanging on the wall in front of me. I cannot tell you how great both of you look. And you are such a *big* boy now! And handsome!

The twinkle in your eyes tells me that you are a mischief-maker, which is something that all little boys should be. That look reflects that you have spunk and a sense of adventure. When I cover up most of the photo and just look at your eyes—well, I can hardly tell the difference between you and Mommy.

Thanks. Thanks. Thanks. You don't know how happy it made me to get the "special delivery" note and photo. And I know that I will be overwhelmed with joy upon my return to Earth when I see you again.

The docking yesterday was quite interesting. Let me tell you how it looked from my vantage, inside the station, await-ing the arrival of my next cosmonaut crewmates.

We had a monitor inside *Mir* that showed the view of us from a camera mounted on the approaching *Soyuz* space vehi-cle. As the *Soyuz* moved closer and closer to the space station, the view of the station began getting bigger and bigger. Then right at the last moment and unexpectedly, things reversed—the station started moving farther away. Another crewmate, who had been watching the approach from a window in a different module, came flying in frantically with the report: "They are pulling away!"

You have to remember that my two cosmonaut crewmates have already been up here on *Mir* for five months. The arriving spaceship is carrying their replacements. The *Soyuz* pulling away was the last thing that they wanted to see.

Within about fifteen seconds of our initial observation, the *Soyuz* stopped moving away and began to approach once again. This time we felt the firm "bump" of a good docking. It turned out that during the first approach the automatic docking system failed to align the two spacecraft—*Soyuz* to *Mir*—so the crew was forced to take over in the manual control mode. They "put on the brakes" and then backed away. The second time Vasily, the *Soyuz* commander, flew the spacecraft into the space station manually. The lesson that I learned from this experience is that while machines are useful, they will never replace us humans totally.

So, now we have quite a crowd aboard *Mir*. Six space travelers from planet Earth. As in any small home, the single bathroom seems to be the choke point. On the other hand, it is nice to see some new faces, hear some new stories, and break up the routine a bit.

Okay, Johnchek. Thanks again for the picture. You and Mommy make me very proud. You are quite the little rascal, I can tell!

Love to you both,
Dad

Hurricane, a Good Bilingual Nickname

Dear John,

It was so nice to see you and Mommy today on the monitor. Although we now have quite a crowd up here on *Mir*, you had even more people in Mission Control–Moscow.

There is something comforting in our seeing all of our families gathered together back on the planet. It helps the crew up here to understand one another more fully, knowing that we all share some of the same concerns. It is also reassuring to see that Mommy has other people down there to turn to who understand completely the feeling of separation.

John, you have acquired a new nickname. After watching you scurry around the television broadcast room, my crewmates decided that you would be called "Hurricane." In Russian, the word sounds about the same, so it is a good bilingual nickname for a boy who speaks bilingual goos.

You take after me. When I was a boy, whenever I misbehaved, my father would make me sit still in a chair for punishment. From my viewpoint, a spanking was a much better alternative. Quick and to the point, the spanking would be complete and I could get back to moving and misbehaving.

But sitting. Tick tock, tick tock. Time would *drag* on. Back then, they had clocks with big hands and little hands that moved ever so slowly around the face of the clock. And I swear that time moved more slowly than on today's digital clocks.

Anyway, my dad would be lying on the couch, taking his fifteen-minute, seems-like-three-hours-to-me lunchtime nap. I knew that if I asked too often if my time were up, he would extend my punishment and make me sit even longer for disturbing him. Mom, who would tell Dad that his naptime was up and that it was time for him to get back to work fixing telephones, more often than not was my savior. I was sure glad that Dad was a telephone man and that he was not unemployed, or his naps might have dragged on forever!

Anyway, "Hooligan" and "Hurricane" are both fine nicknames for a little boy.

Speaking of motion, it has been interesting to note the distinct differences in "flying" around the station between us old-timers and the new crew. The old-timers move gracefully. This is probably attributable to a combination of us knowing the terrain coupled with a total adaptation to the weightless environment. The new guys are clumsy and not yet spacemen. Instead, they more resemble and are still functioning as transplanted Earthlings.

Up here, the three of us who are fully adapted to space fly from place to place by pushing off, very gingerly, and then doing a few midcourse corrections by either bending or twisting slightly. Sometimes, if I find myself deviating significantly from course, I might push ever so gently on a selected fixed object along the way. We brake by again finding a fixed object at the far end of the flight path and reacting against it. Everything along the way—loosely attached cameras, food items, pens and pencils—stayed untouched and in place.

Sasha, Valeri, and I—the old crew—never collide. In fact, we never even touch each other when flying opposed. I am sure that when I first arrived and was not yet fully adapted, they gave me a wider berth than usual when passing. But now we just glide by each other with the greatest of ease. Our personal space is protected without the aid of air traffic control.

Enter the "new guys." There is a huge difference now. Pencils and cameras and gear are flying everywhere! People are propelling themselves off each other. The braking object is the person at the far end of the module. Cords and cables along the flight path become handholds and are constantly being pulled out of their receptacles. But amidst this chaos, I have observed a lessening of this clumsiness as the new guys adapt to weightlessness and learn the more delicate aspects of flying inside a cramped space station.

I suspect that when the space shuttle arrives in May, the situation will repeat itself. By then, my new space station cosmonaut crewmates will have already spent three months onboard and will be flying gracefully and smoothly. The astronauts will appear clumsy and unadapted to them. And when I return to the planet, the Earthlings, long ago adapted to standing upright and walking, will probably look at me and be astonished by my shuffling gait, unsteadiness, and clumsiness. I will have to readapt from spaceman to Earthling once again.

John, I would like to ask of you my first favor. Since this walking thing is something you just learned and is still fresh in your mind, maybe you can give Daddy some pointers after I return. Then we can spend time together just walking, side by side, hand in hand. I would like that.

Goodnight, Hurricane.

Love,
Dad

Crazy House

Kathryn,

As Sasha put it: "It's a crazy house up here." Six people onboard *Mir* at one time is too many people!

Right now I am waiting for breakfast. It takes twenty minutes for the water to heat up. Since the device heats up only enough water to fill the dehydrated food packets for one or two of us at a time, the rest of us have to wait twenty minutes before the next batch of hot water is ready. We grow impatient because the day is so full with work that any delays put us behind schedule.

Communication downlink has been taken up by DARA (the German space agency), as have all available electrical power sockets on *Mir*, so I have been unable to get messages to you or to John. Sorry.

You look great in the photo that the newly arrived cosmonauts brought up! Glad that you have a companion in John. He looks real happy; you are obviously doing a great job with him. My U.S. support team in Mission Control–Moscow says that they had fun playing with him, too. Looks like I am the only one missing out on all of the fun.

I have to go. Comm pass time.

Love you.

J

PS: I started the sleep study last night. Unfortunately, no interesting dreams to report (yuck, yuck).

Physical Training Takes Willpower

Dear John,

Every time that I float by your picture on the wall I smile. You have the happiest look on your face . . . a look that says that you think that life is just grand. Adults only smile like that when they hit the jackpot or, in the case of astronauts and cosmonauts, when they find out that they are next in line for a rocket ride to space.

Let me tell you when I am not smiling: whenever I do my physical fitness training. It is just plain tough up here. I work out two times a day, one hour per session, strapped down to a treadmill. When using the treadmill in the manual mode, I feel like a pack mule trying to haul a cart up a hill. In the powered running mode, I feel as I used to feel running down steep Old Baldy sand dunes at Saugatuck, Michigan. On the sand dunes, I could barely keep my legs moving fast enough to keep up with the downward falling motion of my body. Up here, the treadmill that I use is broken save for one speed: maximum fast. It starts with a jolt and within seconds is turning at full speed. Feet flying, I sprint for dear life in order to avoid being sucked into the treadmill, Fred Flintstone–style. Wilma is not here to save me!

When I am on Earth, I am just like you. I love to stay in motion, love to go to the gym or for a run or even a cross-country ski trip through the Russian woods at midnight. I do it every day out of habit and over the years it has become just as routine with me as brushing my teeth. I never have to talk myself into it; rather, I look forward to workouts. I especially enjoy the reward at the end of a good workout. With muscles aching a bit, I get to relax in a hot and soothing shower.

But up here, it is war. A constant battle to keep the bones from losing their hardness and the muscles from becoming so weak that it would become difficult to stand, let alone run, upon my return to Earth. The pull-down straps of my harness are attached to a load device that not only keeps me from floating but also yanks me down hard. The straps constantly gnaw into my shoulders and hips. Sweat beads up on my skin and carbon dioxide, exhaled but not sufficiently ventilated away, builds up in a bubble around my head. Sometimes the carbon dioxide concentration gets to the point where I feel myself hyperventilating and gasping for air. (There are no breezes up here, no natural convection currents, since warm air does not rise. Fans are not a luxury but are essential to move the stale air toward filters and absorbers.) At the beginning of most of my runs, the soles of my feet feel as if they were being stabbed with pins and needles—so unaccustomed are they to pressure of any kind. (I never "stand" on my feet up here; I only float.) When running, there is no changing view to distract—no passing people or trees or houses, only the same drab cramped module day after day.

This type of running is more akin to doing interval quarter-mile sprints than going for a nice carefree run. I hurt. I grit my teeth and just do it, pushing through the pain.

I have learned some tricks to make running on the *Mir* treadmill more bearable. A heavy and forcefully blown exhale now and then helps to clear the carbon dioxide bubble away from my face, as does directing a fan toward me. The fan also helps to keep me cool and I now keep a towel close at hand to wipe the perspiration.

For distraction, I use a floating CD player and listen to music over my headsets. In the middle of long runs, I sometimes daydream and think about people back home on the planet. To distract further yet, I close my eyes when running and try to visualize places where I used to run on the planet. For example, instead of watching the clock tick down during a three-minute sprint interval, I close my eyes and picture myself running a loop around Bay Area Park. I "see" a baseball game being played, run past the swing sets, wave to the windsurfers, and finally sprint down the street to our home where I see you and Mommy in the front yard. When I once again open my eyes and look back at the clock, I am often pleasantly surprised that even more than the required three minutes have passed and pleased that they were somehow a less painful three minutes at that.

My biggest motivation? When I get home, I want to be able to keep up with you, John! Chase you around the corner and down the hall and into the kitchen, to be rewarded by your big smile and laugh.

The only silver lining to exercising in space is how one feels after the workout is complete. After the session is over and I have squirted myself clean with a packet of water, washed my hair with special astronaut "no-rinse shampoo," and toweled myself dry, I feel great. And then I eat lots and sleep soundly. And I continue to feel human.

Other than those two hours, I am smiling a lot. The work is very rewarding and my crewmates are pleasant and capable. A very supportive NASA mission control team backs me on the ground in Moscow. I am rewarded daily with astonishingly beautiful views of the Earth and cosmos. Finally, the knowledge that you and Mommy, family and friends, and lots of other people back on the planet are behind me, pulling for me, and including me in their prayers, is reassuring. I am a lucky person to be representing you all up here.

Good night, John. Wishing you lots of rapid eye movement with three or four deep-sleep periods tonight. Love you and miss you.

Dad

25 February 1998
A letter to my wife, written after the fire

Safe and Sound

Kathryn,

Incredible, but in the middle of everything I thought of you and John. It helped me.

I love you both very much. Take good care of the little guy. I want you both safe and sound when I finally get home.

Jerry

PS: I can't wait to talk to you. Even the measly three words I was able to hear from you during the last static-filled radio communication sounded good (especially the blueberry pie part, if I heard that correctly!).

Days Fifty through Eighty

Throughout my entire time in space, I was never wanting for things to do. Instead, a day off was something that I craved, but realized was impossible to have, given the amount of work that needed to be done. I was so busy conducting experiments and doing repairs that I hardly had time to think. But whenever I did, I always told myself, "Jerry, this is one incredible opportunity and setting. You are lucky and privileged to be up here doing this work. Do not waste a minute, and do it to the best of your ability."

To be sure, daily life on *Mir* was not one glorious adventure after another, but rather monotonous and confining. We were essentially prisoners: Theoretically we were free, but there was nowhere to go on a Saturday night. Days began to blend into one another. Many of the tasks were repetitious, unpleasant, and, worst of all, seemingly never-ending. It took a great deal of self-discipline to persist.

To my surprise, I never really felt terribly lonely. Cut off, yes. Alone, yes. But memories of people back on the planet always elicited not a hurtful longing, but rather pleasant reminiscences. (My life will be divided forevermore into two distinct categories: life on the planet and life off the planet—the two worlds being so radically different.) Looking out the window always made me realize how incredibly lucky we are to live on such a *magnificent* planet.

Equipment breakdowns continued day after day. The blaring of the master alarm became part of normal life on *Mir*. I consciously tried to avoid burdening my family with my troubles, but at times some of my concerns and fears probably bled through into the letters.

Since my return to the planet, I am often asked, "Was it *fun* up there?" The answer is easy: "No, it was not fun. It was a huge challenge. I am glad that I did it, but my experience could not be described as fun." March 1997 was one of the toughest months of my life.

Good People, Good Friends

Dear John,

How have you been? Sorry that I have not written in a while, but I have been really, really busy doing experiments, preparing for the departure of my first set of Russian crewmates, and fighting fire in between all of that!

Today, we will go to bed at three thirty in the afternoon and get up at midnight in order to prepare for the undocking of the *Soyuz* spacecraft at 0900 tomorrow morning. I would bet that the sleep experiment researchers just love the schedule that I have been keeping: all-nighters and now sleeping during the day. It will most certainly be a complicated, if not interesting, database to analyze upon my return.

Well, I spent a month and a half with cosmonauts Sasha Kaleri and Valeri Korzun, and I can honestly say that we never had a serious argument the whole time. Good people, good friends. I am very happy for them that they will soon be home—six months in space is a long, long time. Sasha has a little boy about your age, John. What a great surprise Sasha is in for. His baby boy was about six months old when he left and is now just over a year. I saw how you changed during that time period of your life (up to the day that you ate your first chocolate cake on your first birthday), and the change was drastic! In fact, I could hardly keep up on your progress and I was there to observe you from day to day. I would love to see Sasha's face when he first sets eyes on his little guy. Mommy said that you will be there when they arrive back at

Star City. Be sure to give them the hero's welcome that they deserve.

Just wanted to say hello, and to tell you that I love and miss you and Mommy. There is a handwritten letter from me for both you and Mommy arriving special delivery on the *Soyuz* via my friends and former crewmates. Yours is the envelope with the balloons, stars, and airplanes sketched colorfully on it. Mommy's is the more serious one. We actually have a post office up here on space station *Mir*, and the envelopes were postmarked today. We'll see if spaceship delivery is quicker than airmail delivery!

Love you, Hurricane.

Dad

2 March 1997
Letter A

Planet Earth Became a Bit More Crowded Today

Hello John,

Well, planet Earth became a bit more crowded today as my two cosmonaut former crewmates and the German researcher returned safely home. You never know who will be dropping in. I heard that they had a good landing in Kazakhstan, landing within 800 meters of their target. They will be back in Star City and into quarantine by suppertime. I am very happy for them and their families.

And in space on the space station, we are back to a three-person crew once again.

We all said good-bye at about two in the morning, then said good-bye again for the cameras at three. The hugs, heart-felt thanks, and good wishes were sincere during both occasions.

As the *Soyuz* departed, I felt nothing inside the space station, not even a gentle nudge. I had some acceleration sensing devices running at the time, so that scientists will be able to quantify the push-off force imparted to the *Mir*. Maybe those sensitive instruments can pick up something, but the effect was below the threshold of my human sensors. In fact, there was less disturbance to the station than when someone runs on the treadmill or a solar panel rotates. (The solar panels rotate in order to catch the sun "full on." When I am strapped to the wall and trying to fall asleep, I can often feel the panels imparting a very low frequency vibration—whoa, whoa, whoa—to the space station.)

My visual sensors (also commonly called eyes, but I am trying to sound like an astronaut!) did catch the *Soyuz* about ten minutes after they undocked. The *Soyuz* capsule was lit up brilliantly by the rays of the sun and stood out starkly against the dark black background of space.

Let me explain why the sun was still lighting up the spacecraft while everything around it, including Earth below, was already in darkness. Interestingly, we fly at a high enough altitude that we still catch rays up here on the station while Earth below has either not quite had a sunrise or already experienced sunset. In other words, Earth below is dark, but we are lit up. During this roughly seven-minute period, an observer standing on the planet can easily see us zipping through the sky, appearing like a shooting star. This is possible only when the observer is looking up near dawn or dusk and our flight path puts us overhead the location of the observer.

The same thing occurred to the *Soyuz*. It passed into an area where it was already dark below, but the spaceship was still catching rays from the sun. From my equally high altitude viewing position aboard *Mir* I could see *Soyuz* lit up for at least ten minutes. I could also see the remaining crescent of light around Earth below growing dimmer and dimmer every minute. I was surprised that I could still see the *Soyuz* through a 300-mm camera lens even when the background turned to stars and the sunset crescent disappeared. And I do not mean the spacecraft's running lights (which I could not see if, indeed, they were on at all), but rather a glow (from reflected moonlight and starlight?) around the vehicle itself. Orion's belt was located right smack behind it. I held steady on the camera and breathed ever so quietly, because with any movement whatsoever, the image would jump from view. I knew that if I lost them for only a moment, I would be unable to spot them again.

When viewed from this great a distance, all the distinct features of the spacecraft were lost. In form, the *Soyuz* looked exactly like a glowing, three-dimensional crucifix, slowly rotating into different orientations. The solar panels were probably the arms. For about a minute I saw the rotating crucifix, until it finally disappeared into blackness. I took the imagery as a good sign.

We were unable to see the reentry of the *Soyuz* into the atmosphere. We all moved to the windows to try to catch a glimpse of the fiery streak of a capsule moving at Mach 20+, feeling the braking force of the atmosphere, and turning into a fireball because of the friction. We finally received word from

Mission Control–Moscow that all went well during the landing. We felt relieved that our friends were safe and sound. Then I went back to my sleep studies. (I find it rather amusing that I can claim to be "conducting experiments," when in fact, I am trying to catch a nap! I like that experiment!)

Okay, John. Mommy said that she is determined to finish up your baby book before she leaves Russia. I am trying to encourage her, because when I return, I want to see what I missed. You will be a little person, not a baby, by the time I get back, John.

Love you very much. Give Mommy one of your special kisses for me. Miss you both. Not too long until I, too, come back to Earth in a fiery streak and we will all be together again. Then, I won't need any more photos, but will have the real thing.

Love,
Dad

2 March 1997
Letter B

Moral Toughness

Dear John,

Even Daddy had to take a nap today. We were up all night preparing for the undocking, so at ten in the morning we were ordered to bed. No complaints from me. Unlike you, I did not cry, stand up and look around, suck my thumb and pout, or squirm around trying to avoid capture. I just smiled and went right to bed. Maybe you can try that sometime. Mommy reports that she is lucky to get you down even once a day. You little hooligan! Life is such an adventure for you and you just hate to miss anything.

John, I want to tell you what I think you should be when you grow up. Mommy's probably worried that I might say fireman, since she knows that I have been playing fireman lately. But that is not the occupation I thought of for you. In fact, what I want you to be is not even an occupation. What I want you to be is honest—a person of integrity. If Mommy and I succeed in instilling in you that one characteristic, I will be satisfied that I raised you well and will be proud of you forever. It would be the ultimate gift that you could give back to me as your father, and by doing it, you would honor me forever. Your actual occupation would be unimportant.

Unfortunately, being honest and having integrity is much harder to accomplish than you might think.

A trauma surgeon in Detroit asked me a good question. He asked if I had any solution to solving the problem of the senseless violence of man against man that he sees the deadly consequences of almost daily in the Detroit hospitals. He asked me, I think, because he knew that I could see the planet as one, without boundary or division, and he thought that with that perspective, perhaps I might have some unique insight. The question has bothered me ever since.

While I don't know the answer, I think that the problem stems from a basic lack of individual honesty, ranging from pretending that prejudice is okay, to rationalizing that it is fine to steal from another person because he has plenty, to somehow justifying killing another person "in this particular instance."

72

It goes on and on; but the common thread is always that people are deluding themselves, being dishonest with themselves.

It takes practice to get good at being honest, John. And determination. And moral toughness. This is because in the short term a little deception, a little lie, makes the road ahead look smoother and easier. But in the long run, dishonesty is always, and I mean always, the wrong path to choose.

I have told you before that your daddy was, in my own father's words, a "scatter-arm." Mommy says that you love playing with any ball that you can get your hands on. If you inherited any of my less than superb throwing ability, someday you will break a window. Imagine that happening, and that no one sees you do it.

You will have an overwhelming urge to wait it out. I mean, maybe someone after you will throw a ball through exactly the same hole. You would then be off the hook.

If confronted directly with the question, "You don't happen to know who broke that window, do you, John?" you will be tempted to say, "No, I sure don't." You might then hope that no witness steps forward and that the name Linenger wore off the ball on its flight through the glass. I would hope that denying the truth would make you feel uncomfortable from the start. Resist the temptation to lie, John.

If someone else is wrongly accused, again it might be tempting to sit by quietly. You could do so and never be directly dishonest. To do the right thing under such circumstances, to speak up, might be especially difficult. You will have to work hard at this to get it right, John.

Even if confronted with evidence—for example, your name written on the ball—you might be tempted cover it up with another little lie by saying something like, "Oh, that is the ball my brother always uses." (Hopefully you will have a brother someday—hint, hint to Mommy!) This illustrates the slippery slope: After you tell one lie, it becomes increasingly difficult not to lie some more. Beware.

In short, John, it is not easy to be honest, to have integrity. Difficult for a child, difficult for an adult. But lies break down trust, and once broken, trust can never be restored.

Don't worry, little guy, you will undoubtedly fib. In fact, I fully expect you to fib. It is part of the learning process. Sadly, perhaps the natural human tendency favors that option. But I will correct you. I will try to explain why it is important to be honest. I will correct you again and again and again. And I will pray that your conscience becomes strong enough so that at the point in your life when you enter adulthood, you will tell the truth even without me standing by to correct you.

If over your adult years, my son, you never falter on this one aspect of life, you will make me forever proud. For my part, I will try to be the best role model possible. And as to concrete occupations, based on my limited experience, I don't recommend becoming a fireman—although the hats, sirens, and Sparky dogs are pretty cool.

Good night John. And good night to the cow jumping over the moon. I'll be watching over you.

Love,
Dad

Human Beings Can Adapt to Space

Dear John,

Was it great talking to Mommy on the radio today! You lucky dog. You get Mommy all to yourself. But pretty soon you will have to share again. Daddy can't wait!

Mommy said you were the entertainment at Alla's birthday party. I understand that you stood in the middle of the room and danced and smiled and laughed and danced some more. You never were shy. And you obviously inherited your rhythm from Mommy.

On the other hand, I would bet that you would be impressed with the gracefulness of your dad now. I can do triple spins with double turns—no problem. I fly with the greatest of ease. My leaps from module to module are a thing of beauty. I sometimes strike the surfer pose—hands out and crouched down low—and slide (fly) sideways through the air. Hang ten.

I was brushing my teeth this morning and started laughing to myself. Actually, I was laughing out loud, but please do not tell that to the psychologists who are keeping an eye on me to make sure that I do not go crazy up here. I realized that I now feel absolutely normal and that half of the time I forget that I am even in space. I do things, like just letting my tube of toothpaste float in front of me, as if I had operated in that manner my entire life. I fly from experiment to experiment as naturally as I would walk on Earth. I just do it without even thinking. As if I were born up here.

The adaptability of the human being is remarkable.

Oh, there are some hiccups. For example, on Earth I can usually eat and go for a run within an hour. I used to love coaxing Cousin Tom into a quick run after dinner and then burying him at the finish because he would suffer a side ache. You will someday be subjected to a stupid rule that you have to sit around and wait for an hour, *a whole hour*, before being able to go for a dip in the lake after lunch. I realize now that that rule had no applicability to me whatsoever, and nearly cost me a happy childhood.

But up here, my digestive system functions differently. If I have something to drink before running on the treadmill, I can feel the fluid "floating up" my esophagus when I run. I am forced to keep re-swallowing. Nothing terrible, but annoying. Actually, I take that back. If I have just drunk a less-than-delicious orange-mango drink, it is terrible to drink it a second time.

Taste changes a bit also. Unlike Mommy, who can eat five-star-hot Thai food and survive, I have never liked spicy-hot food. But although the shrimp cocktail we eat up here burns me all the way to the back of the nose (Is it made of horseradish?), for some reason I now like the taste of it.

Anyway, you get the idea. Subtle differences. In general, human beings can adapt to space just as we have adapted to land. And within a short period of time we can feel entirely comfortable and at home.

I heard that you welcomed back my previous cosmonaut crewmates last night in Star City, Russia. Mommy said it made her cry to see them back on Earth, with me remaining in space. I understand.

Okay, John. Between you and me, I recommend that you do that spit-up trick of yours if Mommy tries to make you drink orange-mango drink. Love you and miss you. Good night. I'll be saying a prayer for you, and watching over you.

Dad

Life in Space Is Never Monotonous

Dear John,

You would think that life on a space station would get monotonous, but so far the opposite is true.

There are new experiments daily: the undocking of our *Progress* supply vehicle, climbing into our launch and entry space suits and flying the *Soyuz* spaceship to a different node, the arrival of the new crew, a fire to get your adrenaline flowing, the departure of my first set of Russian crewmates. And today our unmanned *Progress* resupply spacecraft, now full of our old garbage, returned. Sort of.

Why would we want to bring back our garbage anyway? The first reason is because the exposed docking node on *Mir* gets a lot of direct sunshine. This makes maintaining thermal control on the station difficult, especially with the failure of our cooling system. By physically covering the node with the *Progress*, the *Mir* is essentially "shaded" and thus stays somewhat cooler. Secondly, small but fast-moving particles in space strike the uncovered docking ring directly and erode its surface. Slowly but surely, this bombardment eventually roughens up the surface to the point that it becomes very difficult to maintain an airtight seal with a docked spaceship. For both of the above reasons, it is better to keep the docking ring covered.

Besides these hardware considerations, the overriding reason was to test a manual-approach docking system, called TORU. In the past, *Progress* dockings were always done automatically using sensors mounted on the *Progress*. But those sensors take up room, have weight, and are costly to build. If we could do without them and still successfully dock the resupply ship manually, in the future one could take advantage of the weight savings afforded by not flying the components of the automatic docking system and thus load more cargo aboard each vehicle. Our job was to demonstrate that a docking could be done safely in the manual mode.

The equipment used to accomplish this task included a control panel, a monitor, and two joysticks—all of which were installed by us in the *base block* module of *Mir*. The view that we would see on the monitor inside of *Mir* would be a view of ourselves—the *Mir* space station—taken from a camera mounted on the approaching *Progress* spacecraft. By looking at the monitor and by using the control joysticks located inside *Mir*, but remotely firing the thrusters on *Progress*, Vasily, the *Mir* commander, would drive the *Progress* as if he were inside the approaching spacecraft.

The rendezvous and docking began when the ground sent up radio commands to the *Progress* steering it in our general direction. These commands sent the spacecraft on a trajectory toward us. Once the unmanned spacecraft was within visual range, our job was to then take control and to steer the *Progress* into the exact spot that we wanted it to be—at the docking node. In between the radio commands sent from the ground and before the commander of *Mir* acquired the *Progress* visually, the spacecraft was free-flying on its own—with essentially no one controlling.

Today, we were unable to dock the *Progress* because our TV view was not so great. In fact, the monitor remained static-filled and blank the entire time. Without this sensor information, it was impossible for Vasily to dock the spacecraft since he was essentially flying the spacecraft "in the blind." To be sure, there were some tense moments as the *Progress* zoomed by us and nearly hit us. Hopefully, the smart people down in Mission Control–Moscow will figure out what caused the problem, since we will probably be asked to give it another try in the future. Maybe the failure of the docking today was for the best. I was not really looking forward to opening the hatch of *Progress* and inhaling the smell of our month-old garbage, anyway!

As I said, life in space is anything but monotonous. In fact, I could go for some boring times right now! I think that I will take up fishing when I get home.

I still worry more about you, you little hooligan, than myself. The possibility of you crawling up the stairs and then falling down or putting something into your mouth that is not intended for eating concerns me. Mommy has a full-time job with you, no doubt.

Speaking of Mommy—will you tell her that I love her, miss her, and appreciate all that she is doing . . . alone . . . down there? Geez, she even got stuck doing the dreaded income taxes this year. She is an angel.

Love you John. Praying that you will sleep safe and sound tonight. Mommy, too.

Dad

No Time to Write

Dear John,

No time to write. I did experiments from morning till night, grabbed some dinner, and now need to sleep.

Wishing you pleasant dreams. Kiss Mommy good night for me, please. Love you both.

Dad

7 March 1997

Cry All You Want

Hello John,

Looks like a lot of snow down there in Russia. Have you learned to make a good snowball yet? And can you hit the broad side of the *Prophylactoria* building yet? It will be baseball season by the time that I get back, so you had better start practicing your throwing.

Daddy got his shot today. See, it is not just you that gets all the immunizations; adults have to get shots sometimes, too. And you were thinking all along that it was just something that an adult does to babies and little boys just for the fun of it. In your case, the purpose of the shots is to keep you healthy so that when I come back to Earth we can have a grand time together. In my case, the immunizations are part of an experiment.

Basically, this smart research doctor named Clarence wants to know if the immune response differs in someone who is living in space. He wants to find out whether after an immunization I produce antibodies just like I would back on Earth, or whether my response is altered. If altered, it might mean that after a long period in space I might be more susceptible to infections. The scientists are especially concerned about how space travelers might fare after returning from a long-duration flight and having to once again face the germ pool that you all are brewing in down there. This is the main reason why the cosmonauts stay in the *Prophylactoria* following their flights. By the way, the *Prophylactoria* is that big building in Star City that you can see when looking out the window of our apartment. It's the place where the cosmonaut crew is quarantined before and after each flight. On a more practical level, the building is big enough that you should be able to hit it successfully with a snowball!

No, I didn't cry when I gave myself the shot. But I got to thinking about what was involved. It is a needle. Someone jabs you with it in the arm. You have teensy-weensy arms; so relatively speaking, that needle makes even a bigger hole in your arm. I have decided that I will never again say, "John, when the nice doctor stabs you with a needle, I want you to sit quietly and be nice." Heck, no! Defend yourself; and if the doctor wins out, cry all you want to! It is okay with me, John. You won't shame your father one bit.

To be sure, my pain and suffering are not over yet. This doctor named Clarence now wants someone to draw my blood, which I figure I will do myself since I am the only *real* doctor on board, and who wants a pilot sticking you with needles? I have to do this not once, but periodically over the next month. In addition to the blood, I also insert a cotton plug into my mouth in order to obtain a saliva sample. Then I spin both the saliva and the blood samples in the centrifuge, freeze the samples, and eventually bring them back on the shuttle. So you see, John, you do not have it so bad with those six-month, twelve-month, and eighteen-month stabs! Speaking of which, remind Mommy that it is time for your eighteen-month shots pretty soon. On second thought, I had better tell her myself— you are smarter than that and will, surely, conveniently forget to tell her.

Anyway, I actually had some fun with this experiment today. In the unlikely case I would suffer an allergic reaction to the antigen, my crewmates had to stand by with epinephrine, a respirator bag, and other resuscitation medical gear. I kept saying to them, "Now, remember, if I stop breathing, just relax. Inject this medicine into me, then that one, and if that does not get me breathing, try injecting this one again. Oh, and don't forget, the second medicine goes into the muscle, the first one just under the skin. Then put this mask over my face and squeeze the bag once every second or two. "No big deal," I assured them.

I could see that I had gotten *their* blood pressure up higher than mine. They were sweating and praying that I did not have a reaction to the immunization. In fact, I would venture to say that the commander became more anxious at the prospect of potentially becoming an emergency room space doctor than he was about blasting off into space. I got a kick out of watching him. Hey, you have to do something to entertain yourself up here for five months!

Okay, John, enough of this doctor talk. I think that the doctor named Clarence will probably cook me a nice barbecue when I get back home so that I can rebuild all of my lost blood. And we can play in his pool, smell the aroma of the food cooking, and relax together. I look forward to that.

Miss you. Miss Mommy. Love you both. Take good care of each other.

Dad

8 March 1997

Space Station Is a Five-Star Hotel

Dear John,

I just finished talking to astronaut Ellen Baker on the ham radio. She talked to Mommy in Russia on the phone earlier and passed along Kathryn's love to me as I was zooming over the United States. I will take it any way that I can get it. Pass along my love to Mommy, please.

I am reading a book entitled *Endurance*, by Alfred Lansing. My flight surgeon picked it out. I was pleasantly surprised when, on the first day aboard *Mir*, I opened a bag full of science gear and found the book. I am so tired by the end of the day that I have been reading the book as bedtime reading for two months now and doubt that I will finish the book. My eyes start closing after reading a page.

But my nodding head is not Lansing's fault. The book is interesting reading. Explorers whose goal it was to trek across the Antarctic got trapped in an ice flow and their boat was crushed. They then try to survive living on the ice. Primitive living begins.

Compared to what they endured, the space station looks like a five-star hotel. While they ate seal and penguin meat day after day after day, I feast on Russian and American freeze-dried cuisine: shrimp cocktail, veggies, and borscht—the whole spread. While they faced a winter of darkness, I see light and dark every forty-five minutes. While they viewed gray days and endless white, I look out the window to view the Himalayas, the boot of Italy, and the crook of Cape Cod. While they wore the same clothes for over a year, I get a fresh T-shirt and pair of shorts every two weeks. And while they had to trudge through uneven, unstable terrain, I float effortlessly. In addition, inside of *Mir*, the temperature is controlled, we have electricity, lights, computers, and, every couple of weeks, five-minute talks with our loved ones. My accommodations are not too shabby in comparison to those of these Antarctic explorers.

The book is based on diaries that some of the men kept. In spite of different settings and time periods, there are many similarities in our circumstances. We are both exploring, both feeling isolated, and both enduring hardship. Interestingly, I find that we share many of the same inner thoughts. Here are some of the thoughts that they wrote about that are very similar to what I am feeling now up here on *Mir*.

We both felt/feel a sense of self-reliance, to a greater degree than thought possible. I have come to truly appreciate what others do for me routinely in service, mainly because up here, I am alone. I am the only one around to prepare my meal or mend a broken zipper. The explorers commented that they felt good when they were tested and proved themselves worthy of the challenge. I feel the same sense of satisfaction. Surprisingly, I do not feel longings for home so much, but rather have pleasant reminiscences of times spent there on the planet. They had the same comment. And in general, in spite of everything, I am pretty happy, as were they on the Antarctic ice.

I hope that you and Mommy are happy, too. You have each other. In a couple of months, we will all be together again.

Looking forward to talking with Mommy tomorrow on the radio and finding out all about what you have been up to. It always brings a smile to my face when I hear of your latest trick.

Love,
Dad

9 March 1997
Letter A

Two Beds Are Better Than One

Dear John,

I talked to Mommy today on the radio. It always lifts my spirits when I hear her voice. You were taking a nap. Good boy!

When I was a junior at East Detroit High School, my math teacher handed me a brochure from the National Science Foundation. It listed summer study programs at different universities around the country for high school students. He had marked two that he thought would suit me. One program was at MIT; I forget where the other one was, but it was at an equally humbling place. The brochure stated that the selected students would study advanced theoretical mathematics, utilizing advanced computer systems, blah, blah, blah, blah, blah, and that scholarships were available to those selected.

Well, your father did okay in high school, but I was no geek or nerd. I had no desire to spend my summer indoors studying mathematics.

But the scholarship part sounded promising, so I leafed through the brochure. Your Grandpa Linenger, the telephone man, was trying to put my older siblings, Ken, Karen, and Susan, through college. With Barbara and myself not far behind, I knew that without a scholarship none of the listed summer study programs would be possible for me. After eliminating the suggested math programs, I found a program that was more to my liking: Foresta Institute of Environmental Studies. The brochure stated that the students would conduct field studies in the Sierra Nevada Mountains near Carson City, Nevada. Base camp would be at the Washoe Pines Ranch, but that the majority of the time would be spent in the field, backpacking and conducting environmental studies. Now that sounded like the way to spend a summer!

I applied. They accepted me. I received a scholarship and flew out to Nevada for the summer. And that is where I began to better appreciate the beauty, fragility, and intricacies of our great Earth.

Washoe Pines Ranch, which was formerly a divorce camp, had lots of little cabins for us to stay in. Since Nevada had more lenient divorce laws in the 1960s than other states, many couples would go there to divorce. At that time, it still took two or three days to process all the paperwork, so the women would stay in cabins on one side of the ranch, and the men on the other. Although most of the other students stayed in these rather ramshackle cabins, I ended up sleeping in a teepee. My teepee was located right next to the pee-pee teepee, which consisted of showers and stalls built into a slab of cement and surrounded by a canvas teepee. An interesting setup to say the least and good future astronaut toilet-training indoctrination!

Part of the time was spent on an Indian reservation at Pyramid Lake. The lake was drying up because of irrigation projects further upstream. Water from a river that had formerly flowed steadily into the lake now barely trickled in. Along the shores of the lake, one could see the old waterline etched twelve feet higher on the rocks than the present shoreline. Because of the reduced water level, the salinity increased and the fish died. The Indians lost their livelihood. We were there to help measure and document the changes that were occurring.

Most of the students spread out into the surrounding desert and along the shoreline of the lake. They measured vegetation changes, set traps in order to determine the density of desert rats and other animals, and dodged rattlesnakes. And I mean lots of rattlesnakes. Upon seeing the slithering creatures everywhere, I made up my mind right then and there that I was a natural-born limnologist (the freshwater equivalent of an oceanographer). It was a good decision. My group of amateur limnologists headed out into the lake. I drove the boat. We dropped seiche dishes into the water in order to determine turbidity, took microbial water samples, and measured the salinity level.

All the while, we were being entertained by the frenzied action of our fellow students on the land nearby. We would watch small groups on the shore repeatedly stopping, frozen in their tracks, backing up, and wiping the sweat from their brows after yet another close encounter with rattlers. John, I hope that you inherit Daddy's knack for falling into good jobs.

I can look out the window up here, see only ocean, and know that we will soon be approaching the coast of Africa. Five hundred miles from the coast and the ocean does not appear blue, but rather, dusty brown. Dust storms blowing out of the Sahel and the other great deserts of Africa obliterate my view of the ocean. The Earth observation experts at NASA have told me that this dust actually blows all the way to South America, where it is deposited and enhances the fertility of the land in that continent. Africa's loss, South America's gain. The once great Lake Chad, located in central Africa, now looks more like a smear than a lake, a dusty blotch on the surface of Earth.

The Northern Hemisphere is sparkling spectacularly white. Massive ice flows at the mouth of the St. Lawrence change shape daily. Black soot, residue from burning coal, covers the white snow and distinctively outlines the towns of Siberia and western Canada.

In Amazonia, the jungles are ablaze. I can see literally hundreds of fires burning daily. The rising smoke forms great palls that are clearly discernible from space. Our planet's oxygen-generating jungles are being converted into short-lived farms. What previously appeared as lush, deeply green areas of jungle from my vantage in space are now replaced with brownish-green symmetrical blotches.

As forests along rivers are cut down, erosion dominates. The Betsiboka River now flows muddy brown to the sea from the central mountainous region of Madagascar. And cities throughout the world are easily distinguishable from the surrounding landscape. They look brown and barren.

Still, Earth remains magnificent overall. I enjoyed backpacking and studying the environment that summer when I was a high school junior, and part of the answer to the question of why and when did I decide to become an astronaut is somehow linked to that summer at Foresta Institute. Out on my own. Adventuring. Becoming a bit more self-reliant. And learning to love and appreciate our planet.

Love you, John. I heard that you almost do not fit into your crib anymore, you are growing to be such a big boy. Soon we will all be together again at home in America. You will then have a bigger bed. Your old crib will pass down to your new brother or sister. Two beds are better than one.

Tell Mommy that I love her. Good night.

Dad

9 March 1997
Letter B. A note to my wife

Same, Same in Space

Katya,

Great hearing your voice today. I hope that you are not too wiped out. I know how hard it must be for you. We both need a good, long vacation. (But we both know better, don't we, with baby number 2 coming along!)

Maybe we are now trained, and the sleep deprivation caused by the second baby will be easier to tolerate than with John. What do you think?

There is not a lot to tell you about. I am still up here in space. Same place, same people, same food, and same tread-mill. Arg!

But overall, it isn't too bad. I am sure that in retrospect, when this adventure comes to an end, I will remember it as a great life experience.

Just wanted to tell you that I love you and miss you. Take care, please.

Love,

J

13 March 1997

Good Report on You from Mommy

Dear John,

I sure got a good report on you from Mommy today.

I am impressed with the new things that you can do. Mommy reports that you get her gloves for her when she is leaving the house. You also grab your own boots and gloves when Mommy says, "Okay John, time to go for a walk." At bedtime, you can go and find the peach-apple-pear book from your collection of books when Mommy asks for it, and actually listen to an entire bedtime story without trying to rip out the pages. Coordination-wise, you can walk in the snow and not only crawl up, but also down, the stairs.

When I heard that you broke through some crusty ice and into mud up to your knees, I thought, "Wow, he really must be getting big!" Breaking through ice in Russia in the middle of the winter means your weight must be substantial. Thirty pounds, minimum. Incidentally, my weight is staying about the same up here. I also look about the same and feel about the same. I think that you will have no problem recognizing me when I return.

One change that I have noticed in me: I feel very efficient and competent up here in space.

The competent part may surprise you, but if you saw the varied list of experiments that I am conducting, maybe you would understand why it is difficult to stay on top of all the work. One day I might be looking at microbiological samples, the next day processing metals in a furnace, and the following day observing how flames behave in space. Faced with such an array of varied and complicated work, maintaining self-confidence is no small task. I am up here doing most of the experiments alone. The top-notch specialists who designed the experiments may have spent their entire lives in the specific field of inquiry and worked for years in preparing the specific experiment that I am executing. Yet, it is totally on my shoulders to execute every experiment, in many different disciplines, without mistake.

The opposed-flow flame experiment is a good example. The equipment consists of an igniter coil encircling one end of a cellulose sample, which in turn is wrapped around a ceramic core. Heat sensors probe near the surface, and an oxygen sensor sniffs the air. A solenoid-activated vacuum bottle sucks in air samples during the burning of the cellulose sample. The sample and probes are contained in a miniature wind tunnel, which has a control device, allowing me to vary the rate of airflow over the burning sample. The whole kit and caboodle is inside a sealed, darkened glove box. A shrouded camera peering in over the top of the glove box records the flame propagation. Quite a complicated setup and one that I must execute perfectly each time.

Based on my real-time observations, I am not only doing the required work for this experiment, but expanding on the requirements a bit. For example, by the time I got to the eighth and final flame-test sample today, I had enough feel for the behavior of fire in space to predict that it would not ignite at the prescribed airflow rate. This is an important piece of information in and of itself, so I ran the wind tunnel at this rate initially. But I also slowed the photography interval rate in order to buy the time to later increase the flow rate and thereby observe whether the cellulose sample would ignite at the higher flow.

A programmed machine could not do that. Only a trained human observer, a scientist, can use his or her judgment to improve the data yield of the experiment. Modification of the protocol based on human observation, evaluation, and intervention provides the scientists on the ground with better data and better understanding of the nature of flame propagation in space.

John, you are already honing your skills of observation and integration of knowledge. When you can pick out the peach-apple-pear book, it shows that you, too, are a good observer, a good assimilator of information. When I get home, we will spend lots of time together, with you showing off your new-found skills to your father. You make me so proud, John.

Love you. Enjoy your bedtime story and pleasant dreams. Give another kiss to Mommy for me, please. I'll be watching over you.

Dad

We Move Fast

Dear John,

Well, it is college basketball playoff time. Although I am in space far away from the bouncing balls, I have made my picks. I pick my alumni, the North Carolina Tarheels, to go all the way. Even though Mommy probably has not even seen the brackets, I bet that she picked Duke, Carolina's nemesis.

Cousin Tom out in San Diego always took selecting the winners of the tournament seriously. He would study the team stats, examine the end-of-season trends, and look at the rankings. Then he would make his choices.

Mommy would pick the teams based upon whether she liked the name, knew someone who went to that university, or knew that the team was the archrival of the team that I was rooting for. In the end, tallying up the wins and losses, she usually outpicked both Tom and me. It would burn Tom up.

With Coppin State, Tennessee-Chattanooga, and St. Joseph's PA all winning in the first round, well, I would bet that one could just throw darts randomly at a bracket listing and beat us all!

We have a ham radio up here. We move so fast—17, 000+ miles per hour—that we can only talk a bit with the people below on the planet. A typical conversation might sounds like this:

Me: "KC5HBR, Kilo Charlie Five, Hotel Bravo Romeo, aboard space station *Mir*, CQ, CQ."

The KC part is my ham radio call sign, and CQ means that I would like to talk with someone out there listening. I throw in the *Mir* part because, believe me, all operators on the ground would drop whatever they are doing in order to make contact with someone in space. In fact, it is considered a real feather in their cap.

Some insomniac in Seattle: "KC5HBR, this is Yankee Zulu (static static static) two."

Me: "Yankee Zulu something, I could not hear it all due to breakup, good morning." Glancing out the porthole, I notice that it is dark down below, so I correct myself, saying, "I mean good day." (I might sound like Paul Harvey or an Aussie, but "goodday" covers all the bases.)

The Seattle guy, responding: "Wow! This is the first time I ever got through to the space station! How are you doing up there, KC5HBR? I read about the fire. Are you guys okay?"

Me, trying to get to the point: "Oh, fine. Hey, Yankee Zulu, you don't happen to know if Carolina beat Fairfield last night, do you?"

The Seattle guy: "Oh, yes! I love college basketball. It was a great game. In the final seconds, they (static, static) . . . ."

Me: "Yankee Zulu, you were broken, say again please."

Nothing but more static.

Then, some other guy in Topeka, Kansas, who is now picking me up as I zoom overhead: *"CQ Mir, CQ Mir."*

He might have time to tell me how his beloved Kansas Jay-hawk team did, but his voice is drowned out by static by the time he gets around to telling me how Carolina fared.

Then a Florida guy, then we fly off into the Atlantic. We move fast.

I told Jay, another ham radio operator in Los Angeles, that I liked the Tarheels. The next day on packet (a machine that listens and can receive email-like messages from ham operators), I read a complete story of how Dean Smith (Carolina's coach) had broken the record for most wins ever for a college basketball coach.

Jay came through. He went through all of that trouble for me. People are okay, John. He figured that he could do something nice for me and took the time to do it. Kindness and thoughtfulness, given freely.

All right you rascal—off to bed. Enjoy your bedtime story. Love you and miss you, John. Good night.

Dad

18 March 1997

Early Explorers Never Talked to Their Loved Ones

Dear John,

Sorta talked to Mommy on Sunday. At least I heard her voice a few times.

We move fast. The station rotates. The antenna is not always aligned. Only a few ground antenna stations are now operating in Russia due to the country's financial woes. The

Russian phone system is outdated. Our transmitter on board *Mir* that aims our signal toward a satellite is broken. Combine all of that and the chance of me having a normal conversation with Mommy adds up to about zero. We have averaged less than five minutes of intelligible conversation a month.

On the other hand, who can complain? Early explorers never talked to their loved ones. Sometimes, if they were lucky, they might receive a three-month-old letter by boat. Although email is rapidly taking over, mail call on U.S. Navy ships is still a big deal. So tolerating prolonged periods of time without being in contact with love ones has been done and can be done.

The problem is really one of expectation. I read the entry "Private family conference, bort engineer USA (that's me), at 1645" on the schedule. I set my wristwatch alarm to the prescribed time. I look forward to hearing Mommy's voice, her laugh. And, of course, the latest John progress report: Mommy informing me of what you have been up to lately and all of your new accomplishments. When the time comes, I am all smiles, anticipating hearing Mommy's sweet voice. Instead, I hear static and an occasional word or two. Usually, only a very distant and garbled, "Jerry, do you hear me?"

I come away from the conversation feeling worse off, a bit lonely, and somewhat cheated. Although the poor communication is no one's fault, it hurts me nonetheless. And Mommy, too, I suspect.

Everyone asks me about loneliness, about how I cope with being alone and in space for five months.

The short answer is that the loneliness, though felt, is not crippling. The reason that I tolerate it so well, I think, is that I prepared myself for it. Even before the flight, I did a little test.

On January 1st, a year ago, I played a game with myself, saying, "Okay, Jerry, pretend you are in space starting today." In May, I told myself, "Okay, you are now back home again." It was a long time. John, you changed tremendously over those five months and I really, really enjoyed watching you go from baby to toddler. I knew that I would miss a lot. But I also determined for myself that yes, I could tolerate a separation of that length.

I work long, long hours every day. The work gives me a great sense of accomplishment, of achievement. I feel worn out, but I also feel that I am doing something for my country. I say that very sincerely: Personal sacrifice for my country is worthwhile sacrifice, and is warranted. The sense of accomplishment is personally rewarding. It helps me. I do not whine, I do not sit (or float!) in a corner and tell myself how miserable it is without pretzels, without trees, without family. No, I keep my chin up and carry on.

When I think of you, Mommy, and other loved ones, it gives me a good feeling. When I fly by your picture on the wall and see your smile, it makes me happier than I was the moment before I looked. I write to you because it brings you to me, and me to you and Mommy. When writing, I relax a bit, feel content, and look forward to returning. Thoughts of home are good thoughts, neither a preoccupation nor something painful.

Anyway, we are luckier than the explorers of old. My letters usually reach you within a week. I know in my heart that Mommy cares for me and misses me. I don't really need to hear the words. She is very special.

Love you, John. Pleasant dreams. I'll be thinking of you and watching over you.

Dad

All Alone in a Dark Room

Dear John,

I heard from Mommy that you have been restless at night. Keeping Mommy up every two hours or so. Maybe you just want some company. Being all alone in that dark room can be a bit frightening for a little guy. Or a big guy, for that matter.

Last night it got really, *really*, really dark in my room— module *Spektr*. We lost all electrical power. I have been in dark places before, but this was un-Earthly dark. Darker than any dark I had ever seen. In fact, the word "dark" is not adequate to describe what I saw.

And silent. So silent. Until then, I had not realized that on board *Mir* we are constantly being bombarded with the noise of turning ventilators and machinery. The silence was unfamiliar and even a bit surprising. For a moment I thought, "What is that (that I don't hear . . .)?" Once recognized, the silence was a very soothing and pleasant lack of sound. Silence sounded nice.

Of course, I could not hang out in the dark, quiet room. No ventilators working equate to no air circulating. Warm air does not rise in space—which way is up? There is no natural convection, no wind and no breeze. Without the ventilator fans working, there is only suffocating stillness.

In fact, because there is no natural convection, we cosmonauts and astronauts always pick a place to sleep where we can feel some air movement near our heads. Without air movement, we will find ourselves enclosed within a self-generated carbon dioxide bubble, waking up panting for air. More likely than not, the air hunger is accompanied by a headache. By the way, the reason why I sleep upside down on the wall is because in the particular place where I sleep the ventilation is better near the floor. I want my head located there by the "good" air.

So John, close your eyes and sleep. The peace, quiet, level of darkness, comfort of your crib, fresh air, and secure feeling of being at home all make for a good night's sleep. Mommy and I will be watching over you. Rest well and grow healthy.

Love,
Dad

22 March 1997

Watching from the Sidelines

Dear John,

I notice that it is the twenty-second of March today.

Twenty-two was always my number. Football, baseball, basketball, whatever—if I had a choice, I would choose number 22. It sounds good, twennty-toooo. And it looks good, too, with its nice repeating curves. Who wants number 68? Or 53? No ring to 'em.

For some reason, the number on my back was important. And when the announcer said, "Tackle by number 22 of the Tigercats, uh, Line-gar" (or Lenin-gar, or Lean-jer, but never pronouncing it correctly: Linen, like the white cloth—you know: linen!—ger), well, I was proud to hear my number called even if my name was mispronounced.

I bet that someday, John, you will have your own favorite number. And I guarantee people will stumble over pronouncing your last name. If they have problems pronouncing "John," either you are in a different country or you should politely move along and start conversing with someone else!

When you do get your chosen number someday, I will be on the sidelines yelling, "Way to go number umpty-ump." Or just quietly watching, being there for you.

I still remember my dad (your Grandpa Linenger) always being there, cheering me on. Always. What I would not give to have him back now.

During my first launch on shuttle, the weather was lousy. We sat on our backs in space shuttle *Discovery* for two hours past the scheduled liftoff time, hoping that the weather would clear. Then just before it was time to call it quits and scrub the launch, the clouds opened up just enough to allow us to take off. My mom said that she saw a rainbow appear at that moment.

My launch to *Mir* was at night. A perfectly clear, spectacularly dark night with billions and billions of stars out. We lit up the sky precisely at the planned launch time. People watching said that they could see the solid rocket boosters being jettisoned at two minutes and then us burning the three main orbiter engines well beyond that time. My mom said that just as we went out of sight, she saw a brilliant shooting star flash across the sky.

She is certain that my father is still watching from the sidelines.

Good night, John. Love you. I'll be watching over you.

Dad

Who Needs Maps?

Dear John,

Mommy said that Tony Sang cooked up some spicy Chinese food today for all the Americans living in Star City, and that you just gobbled it up. You have inherited Mommy's taste buds, no doubt. She orders food five-star spicy and then requests some extra hot sauce on the side. Not me. That type of food burns my mouth and causes an instant, body-drenching sweat.

Let's make a deal. When I am home and we have spicy food for dinner, I get dibs on your bottles of mashed-up peas, applesauce, and pureed turkey. You can have my hot tamales. Agreed?

I had a good day up here today. I ran some experiments in a furnace that is itself "levitating" on an isolation mount. I am trying to prepare pure metal alloys so that we can better ascertain the exact diffusion coefficients of different metals.

The furnace is a neat little gadget and reminds me of the Easy-Bake oven that my sisters used to cook in. I set it up properly and then watch it do its thing.

A pencil-sized metal sample automatically zips into the oven compartment of the device where it bakes for four hours or so. The sample is then extracted and is quenched by two cold metal plates that move in from both sides. Then sample number two automatically zips into the adjacent furnace and the process repeats. I keep an eye on the oven to assure that the sequence is proceeding as planned.

At the end of the experiment run, I download all of the data, temperature readings mainly, into a computer. After connecting cables, I then transfer the data to a data storage device called a WORM. I have lots of WORMs up here just full of data, since the American science program experiments have been very successful thus far. Sometimes I run analysis programs that plot nice curves and other pretty pictures. If I see sine waves that resemble wiggling worms, this is a good sign. By further studying the plots, I can determine if all is functioning properly and, if not, make adjustments on the next batch of samples.

I then send subsets of the data to the smart people on the ground. Tony Sang, the cook whom you like so much, being one of them. They then tell me things like, "The floater accelerations are lagging a bit behind the stator in the z-axis. Better run program umpty-ump." I promptly respond: "Of course, that was so obvious from the plots! I was just about to do that! That was *some* kind of curve, wasn't it?" Usually, I can fool them, since we talk over the radio and I don't have to look them directly in the eye.

Radiation wreaks havoc on electronic devices, so we need to be careful about how and on what media we store data. It is wise to store the data on different types of devices. If one source becomes corrupted, the other may still work.

Camera film and radiation are not the best of friends, either. We test different film types to see which suffers the least when exposed to the radiation environment up here on *Mir*. Slow, color-positive film seems to hold up the best, so that is the type of film that I use to shoot selected sites on the planet. I hope that the film holds up well, because someday I would like to show you some of those photos of our planet, John. You can take them with you to geography class. Who needs maps?

Radiation does provide a pretty good light show at night, though. When I close my eyes, every now and then I will "see" a flash streaking across my field of view. It is caused by a cosmic particle penetrating my eyelid and then striking and exciting the nerves on my retina. If it strikes dead on, I see a small but brilliant dot. If it strikes as a glancing blow, I see a linear contrail moving across my field of vision. The flashes are especially strong and frequent when we fly over the South Atlantic, where an "anomaly" exists. The South Atlantic anomaly is a defect in the protective magnetic belts (Van Allen belts) that surround Earth. When *Mir* passes through this anomaly, we become exposed to a greater concentration of cosmic radiation and the frequency of the flashes increases.

Well, enough for now. This science stuff is fantastic, and I am lucky to be a part of it.

Someday, John, we will work together with your chemistry set and maybe I can show you a thing or two. If someone doesn't invent a "new math 2" by then, I may even be able to help you with your homework. (Anyone who grew up in the late sixties was hopelessly out of luck getting any help with their math homework because some wise guy thought up this thing called new math. It totally baffled every parent alive at that time. Although my dad could always give me the answer to the math problem, he could never tell me which side of the equal sign to put the Xs and Ys on!)

Okay. Good night my future chemist/engineer/whatever you choose. Love you. Miss your mischievous smile.

Dad

Pain Helps Imprint Things

Dear John,

Another good day up here in space. It is amazing how much one person can do in one day. By the end of the day I can hardly remember what I did first thing in the morning. (Today, I remember, though: I drew my blood. Pain helps imprint things a bit more firmly, I suppose.)

I heard that you are going on a trip. Traveling is great, and you always loved heading off with Mommy and me, no matter where we took you.

At first, I held you in a front-mounted infant carrier, keeping you under my big blue down-filled coat to protect you from the Russian winter. You would just snuggle up and sleep. I would peek in now and then to make sure that you were safe and sound. Here is what I remember of St. Petersburg: the Hermitage, strolling Nevski Prospect, and eating ice cream cones as we walked along the street. (Hey, everyone was eating them even though it was freezing outside. Mommy and I ate them and shivered just like the Russians!) What you remember of the trip is probably more akin to bouncing up and down inside a blue, cloth-lined cave—the inside of my coat!

As you grew bigger, you graduated to a position on my back. Man, you loved it up there, sitting in the infant backpack, looking around at the sites and pulling on my ears as if they were the reins of a horse. And whenever you saw a dog, you would let out a woof-woof sound and your eyes would grow big and light up. Your baseball hat never stayed on your head for more than two or three minutes, unless I could distract you somehow. Czar John, we would call you, all perched up on your throne.

Well, I am traveling alone now . . . more than twenty-five million miles and counting. I could carry you all day up here; you would be as light as a feather. And if you stopped your habit of pulling on my ears, I would not even know that you were resting on my shoulders.

Back on Earth, after carrying you around all day, I would be worn out by the time that we got home. By then, I could feel your tired little head plopped down on the back of my shoulder. I would pull you out gingerly from the backpack, lay you in your crib, cover you up, and say a little prayer for you.

Good night, John. Although I won't be able to cover you up tonight, you will still be in my prayers, as always.

Dad

25 March 1997

Ohio River Flooding

Dear John,

It is rather strange. I come to the computer every night with absolutely no idea what I will write to you about. Let's see . . . .

Today I was busy dawn to dusk. Of course, that expression does not exactly apply up here. Since we have a sunrise and sunset sixteen times a day, that would imply that I was busy for only about forty-five minutes. I was cooking metal samples in my Easy-Bake oven, cleaning filters, trying to take some photographs of the flooding down along the Ohio River, and running computer programs in order to archive the great deal of data that I have already collected up here.

Oh yes, one cannot get away from chores, even in space. We vacuum, wash down the walls with towels soaked in a special fungus-fighting solution, and generally straighten things up every Saturday morning. Anything that flies, which means anything not carefully fastened by Velcro or placed behind elastic cords, usually finds its way to the intake filters of the ventilators. In addition to the air circulation fans, just about all of our science gear contains small cooling fans. Without them the air would just stagnate and the temperature within the device would build. So cleaning all the fan intakes is quite a project.

When vacuuming, I always carry a lost-and-found bag for all the goodies that I gather. During the week, I never declare anything truly lost until after Saturday morning, since missing pens, tools, diskettes, toothbrushes, you name it, can usually be found in the filters. The items are merely "displaced" and "out for a fly" when they disappear during the week. Each Saturday morning they are returned home.

The vacuum we use resembles a small-sized, tubular-shaped one that you might find back on the planet. It has a hose in the front and exhausts out of the back. The vacuum is actually fun to use. I fly around with it tucked between my legs, and by having the exhaust pluming aft, I can use it to propel myself along the way. It is essentially a makeshift thruster.

As to photographing the Ohio River, all that I could see

were clouds from the Mississippi to the East Coast, but interestingly, the clouds spread out in a very fine line along the coast itself, north to south. The beaches alone were sunny. It did not appear to be the kind of day that the flood victims along the river were hoping to have down there.

I had a special radio session with Mommy last night because it was our six-year wedding anniversary. Before I left, I prearranged to have flowers sent to her on special occasions. She received the flowers. She said that they were nice. We told each other that we love each other and miss each other. I told her that I really got lucky to snag a woman like her. She laughed.

In the background, I could hear you jumping up and down on the bed and laughing. So it sounds like all is well. I slept content.

Good night, John. You lucky dog, you get to be with Mommy. Sleep tight.

Dad

26 March 1997
Letter A

One Wristwatch Is Not Enough

Dear John,

I am waiting for a computer to finish downloading data, so I have a moment.

Most of your letters have been written in snippets. It is unusual if my wristwatch alarm does not go off at least once during the writing of a letter, disrupting my session. Usually, it reminds me that I need to check on something, activate or turn off an experiment, or do some other task. If I do not get around to writing the letter until late at night, it is always a struggle just to keep my tired eyes open.

Up here I always wear two wristwatches. I have not taken off either of the watches the entire time that I have been up here. One wristwatch alarm is not enough. To stay productive, I need to have at least three things going at once. I fly from one task to another, pretty much nonstop. I squeeze the daily runs, bicycling, and meals in between the work, because every minute is taken up. By the end of the day, I am ready to pass out.

I plan on not wearing a watch at all for a while after I return. I want to play with you and talk to Mommy (and play with Mommy a bit, too!) bare-wristed and without interruption. No alarms to mold my day into artificial parts.

One of the alarms has just starting ringing. I told you! It is time to get back to work on the microgravity isolation mount and download the data. Enjoy your splendid, carefree frolicking, John. Love you.

Dad

26 March 1997
Letter B

About Your Dad

Dear John,

I am trying to catch my breath. I just saw the spectacular site of huge, icy-blue glaciers flowing through the Andes and into the bluer than blue Lake Viedma, Argentina, near the southern tip of South America. Today was a rare, perfectly clear day over the glacier. Whenever I see the wonders of Earth like that my heart races. I think to myself, "How lucky can I get? I have a splendid view of our planet right out the window."

I get almost as excited as you get when you see Mommy walking into the house from outside. Not quite, but almost. I can picture you clearly: flapping your arms, running toward her faster than your legs can carry you, huge smile, big eyes, and so excited that you sometimes forget to let your breath out. I had that same kind of feeling.

John, I have been gone for a while. Sometimes I think that maybe you have forgotten about me. But I heard that whenever you walk down the corridor outside of the NASA office in Star City, Russia, and see my picture hanging on the wall, you stop, point at the picture, and say, "Mommy." That's accurate enough, John. Even more heartwarming for me is when you approach that picture, on your own and without prompting, and give that photo of me a kiss. That makes me feel even better. Thanks.

About your Dad, to refresh your memory.

I am pretty serious and oftentimes grouchy-looking. In fact, the first impression that Mommy had of me was that I was not very friendly. This may surprise you because I smile a lot, as all proud fathers would, when I am around you.

I work hard and am focused. I do not leave things unfinished and I expect others to do their part. I despise mediocrity, especially when I know that through harder work things can be improved. I work very methodically when a task is important. I can be counted on and am always dependable.

Self-discipline is my strong point.

I love our country. I have been serving in our U. S. Navy for almost twenty years now. A couple of years ago, Mark Clark, my former Annapolis roommate, and I were walking from his classroom at Michigan State University. I had just talked to his freshman English class about space. Michigan State has a classic campus—tree-filled with a meandering river—and it was a fresh-air kind of day. Along the way I picked up a small piece of litter and tossed it into a waste container.

When on the following day Mark's class discussed my visit, he told them that Jerry Linenger truly and sincerely loves his country. He told the class that the answer that I had given them to their question concerning my reasons for wanting to become an astronaut was sincere—that part of the reason was, indeed, out of a sense of duty to serve our country. He then told them about my going out of my way to pick up a piece of litter and suggested that that simple act exemplifies the sincerity of that love. Maybe so.

I have incredibly good luck. I win at Monopoly, spoons, or rock-paper-scissors nine times out of ten. I never land on Boardwalk unless I own it. I am not the person that you want to be pulling a wishbone with. In fact, I now wish that the other person will get the long part so that he or she might have a chance to have a wish come true now and then. If I don't make that particular wish, I inevitably end up with the big half of the bone.

When you get to know me, I am all right. When you get to know Mommy, she is the greatest. Since I hang around with her I have friends and get lots of dinner invitations. Although I recognize that I am not the main attraction, at least I am a tolerable, neutral sort.

I eat enough for three or four people. I have been told countless times, "Wait until you hit age umpty-ump and you will have a weight problem." But I am still skinny by my mom's and grandmother's reckoning, just about dead center in the desirable height-weight charts. No waistline creep yet.

That is enough for now, John. To make it simpler for you to recall who I am, I am the guy that used to carry you on my back, throw you balls, chase you around the house, and change your bad diapers. (Somehow, it is always my turn when the aroma indicates that it is clearly not going to be a fun diaper change.) And I am looking forward to doing the same once again not too long from now.

Good night. Pleasant dreams. Give the "other" Mommy a kiss for me, please.

Dad

27 March 1997

Halle-Bopp and the Lonely Moon

Dear John,

Today I will have an interview with WCBS-New York. The interviewer will be Mr. Harley Carnes, the afternoon anchor.

Do people change their names to fit their jobs, or are they destined at birth to do certain types of work? Harley Carnes. The name just sounds like someone who would be on the radio. One of the astronauts is named Brent Jett. John Bartmann Linenger. Hmmm . . . I am not really sure that I could predict your future based on your name, John!

I saw Halle-Bopp today. The comet looks like a shining flashlight against the dark background of the night. There is nothing subtle at all about the comet. Instead, it just screams at you: I am out here now and I will see you again in two thousand years.

But the comet was not the main attraction in the sky. The Northern Lights were going ballistic! Huge green plumes were streaking up from along Earth's northern limb. Amoeba-like, always changing and dancing, electric with energy. And sweeping across the entire northern horizon.

A moment later, I looked down through a different window facing Earth. Although it was dark on the planet below, I could make out the outline of Lake Winnipeg. The distinctive finger of land was cutting into the lake from the west and the city lights of Winnipeg were shining to the south.

Out of yet a different window, the Moon. Lonely looking—alone and by itself.

The sun then began to subtly light up the thin rimming line of atmosphere curving around Earth directly in front of our flight path. The atmosphere appeared as a thin, fragile band, ever so narrow. As more light from the Sun filtered through the ring of atmosphere, the band bloomed into a rainbow of colors. As the Sun rose still higher, it finally pushed its way out from behind Earth. The direct light from the Sun was so absolutely blinding white that I had to quickly turn away.

Just another day in space.

What got me to the window in the first place was the fact that, at that time, we began using a sensor to gather data on stars. The space station was in "inertial attitude" (yes, attitude, not altitude), which means that we were staying stable relative to the stars. We would find a predetermined star, align the crosshairs of a sensor over that star, and then keep the star centered in the crosshairs by continually adjusting the attitude (orientation) of the space station. It was a great opportunity for me to observe the dynamics between Earth, the Sun, and the cosmos.

Sleep tight. The Halle-Bopp comet will be shining for you tonight. No need to turn on a night light. Love you, John.

Dad

PS: Halle-Bopp—there's another almost predestined name combination. It *sounds* like a comet, doesn't it? I think that I am on to something, John Bartmann Linenger.

28 March 1997

Two Trips in One

Dear John,

My NASA Ops Lead just informed me that my time in space has now exceeded that of the *Skylab* astronauts. Man, they sure were up there a long time!

I have actually had two stays on this space station; separated by a fly-around aboard the Russian *Soyuz* spacecraft. I arrived, then left, arrived again, and am now waiting to leave once more, this time aboard the space shuttle *Atlantis*, in May. That trip will make my mode of transport, in order: shuttle, *Soyuz*; *Soyuz*, shuttle. If all goes as planned, I will also make one other "side trip": leaving inside of my Russian Sokol space-walking suit and returning five hours later. It is always nice to break things up—two long-duration missions rolled into one.

From Samuel Butler, in *Erewhon*: "Exploring is delightful to look forward to and back upon, but it is not comfortable at the time, unless it be of such an easy nature as not to deserve the name." What I am doing is truly exploring and deserves the name.

I hope that you and Mommy are enjoying your mini-Easter vacation. Keep your eye on your red jellybeans—Mommy's been known to snitch 'em. Recommend that you offer up the black ones.

Happy Easter, John.

Love,
Dad

29 March 1997

What I Miss

Hello John,

People often ask me what I miss.

You and Mommy, of course. Likewise, family and friends.

But I also miss fresh air blowing in my face. Green, green grass and swaying trees. Birds chirping. Tulips popping up in spring.

Taking hot showers. Lying on the couch. Falling asleep with two big pillows surrounding my head. Diving into the swimming pool after a long, hot run.

Tinkering in the garden. Looking out over the lake as the sun sets. Feeling the warmth of the sun. Gliding across the water in a kayak with fish jumping in my wake.

Pretzels. The smell of popcorn, or better yet, homemade bread baking. Dinner conversations with Mommy. Cuddling.

Silent nights. Crickets. Waves pounding on the shore. Walking barefoot in the sand. Walking. Holding hands.

Basically, I miss the elemental things of Earth that we are blessed with each day on the planet but often take for granted.

After I land, my eyes will be opened as wide as yours always are, John, as I rediscover the little pleasures. Father and son, holding hands and out adventuring together.

Rest up. We will be busy together. Good night.

Love,
Dad

30 March 1997

The Northern Lights

Dear John,

How is our little traveler? You put in almost as many miles as your father, with all of your traveling. I hope that by now you are once again home safe and sound.

Every so often up here, we get stuck in an orbit that seems to keep taking us over land masses during the period of time when it is nighttime on the planet below. When we sleep, the interesting spots below are having their daytime. Therefore,

115

during our waking hours we see only oceans. Oceans are vast and islands are pinpoints. In between the islands are long stretches of water and clouds, not all that interesting to observe. So during these periods of poor Earth observation opportunities, I turn my attention toward the heavens.

The Moon is just incredible. Looking through binoculars, the surface is crystal clear. I actually wiped my eyes a few times in disbelief the first time I looked at it because the shadowing off the crater rims was so distinct. I could distinguish between the high and low places, as if I was looking at a lunar topographical chart.

When I use the "Big Dog" binoculars, the Moon fills the entire field of view. It's not dissimilar to looking down on the Himalayas in shadow. The mare, craters, and even astronaut John Young's Moon Rover tire tread tracks, are visible. (Okay, I am exaggerating on the last point.) If mankind had some settlements there, I am quite certain that I could pick them out as easily as I pick out the cities on Earth below.

I have already spoken of the wonders of the Northern Lights, but today they surprised me once again. Near each of the extreme ends of the curved horizon was a dark "cliff." Pouring off the cliffs was a "waterfall" of greenish, ever-changing plasma. In the foreground, I could actually see a ring connecting the waterfalls and circling the top fifth of the planet.

Unfortunately, photographing these types of phenomena is tough to do up here. I would need some very fast film, which I do not have. In the high radiation environment of space, high-speed film degrades too rapidly to be used during long-duration flights. Aboard the shuttle, with shorter on-orbit duration times, astronauts do carry higher-speed film and have taken some very good photographs of the Northern Lights. I have resorted to making some sketches of what I have observed. I also make a mental effort to imprint the scenes and dynamism as firmly as possible in my brain.

Well, I've got to fly. (This is the space-talk equivalent of the phrase "I've got to run.") I have a radio communication session scheduled where, hopefully, I will be able to talk with my brother and sisters back in Michigan. I will be wishing them a Happy Easter.

And happiest of Easters to you and Mommy. I love you both. I am sure that the Easter bunny will hop through the Russian snow and find your basket, John.

Love,
Dad

31 March 1997

Great-Grandma

Dear John,

Tomorrow is your Great-Grandma Pusavc's birthday. She will only be ninety-one years older than you are presently.

I heard that she baked pateetsa for Easter. (I don't know how to spell it, but I sure know how to eat it!) She made the dough, crushed the nuts, rolled the dough out with a wooden roller, and then baked loaves. After twelve hours of baking, when talking with your Grandma Linenger on the phone, she said with her ever-present Slovenian accent, "Geez, Frances, I am feeling a little bit tired."

However, she then proceeded to walk to evening Mass, returning at ten at night.

Your great-grandma is amazing. She can remember the birthdays and wedding anniversaries of all of her children and grandchildren and great-grandchildren. And it is quite a flock. If I were as smart and sharp as she is, I could tell you the exact number of each category; but I am not, and I can't. Grandchildren alone would have to total more than twenty. Remembering all of their names is challenge enough for me.

She says things like, "Jerry, remember back on June 21st, 1986, when we ate at that nice restaurant in Old Town, San Diego, and I bought you that jumbo margarita?" I have learned to not challenge a thing she says, because she is always right. My reply, "Of course, that was a great June 21st, 1986, wasn't it Grandma?"

So John, remind Mommy to give Grandma Pusavc a call and to relay my greetings. Although she has done a lot in ninety-two years, I do not think that she has ever received a birthday greeting from space before.

Happy Birthday, Grandma. From your grandson, Jerry. Birthday: 16 January 1955. Wedding anniversary: March . . . 20 something . . . it was winter, I am quite sure . . . 24th, was it?

Love you, John. My hope is that your own life will be as fulfilling as Great-Grandma's has been.

Dad

Days Eighty through One Hundred Ten

Yes, I believe that I am a changed person because of my experience in space. The most profound change that I have noticed is my changed sense of perspective.

My grandmother and grandfather emigrated from Slovenia to America in the early 1900s. Formerly a part of Yugoslavia, Slovenia is now a small independent country, a country not often photographed from space. Given my roots, I decided to brush up on the geography of that section of Earth and to do a concentrated study of the region through space photography.

Since the boot of Italy looks like a boot, it is a good orienting landmark for the region. The Adriatic Sea sparkles deep blue, with mountains rimming its eastern shore. The Italian city of Trieste stands out near a diamond-shaped piece of land on the northern reaches of the Adriatic. Stretching northward to the Austrian Alps is the country of Slovenia. The entire region is a gem.

I would occasionally receive news summaries, beamed up to the *Mir* via radio telemetry. I read an article about the continued, never-ending fighting in Bosnia on the same day that I had photographed the region extensively. From my perspective in the heavens, I could see no boundaries below, no artificial divisions, only beautiful mountain ranges. That the people of the planet would be slaughtering one another for *whatever reason* made no sense. "What are they *doing* down there," I wondered. It seemed so utterly senseless.

The broad perspective is one that would serve us all well. When finding oneself in the midst of a conflict, large or small, take a step back. If the problem still cannot be understood, step back farther. I can attest to the fact that given a broad enough perspective, all conflicts appear senseless. We are all in it together on planet Earth. We are not separate. There are no true divisions between us, only those that we artificially impose.

To any astronaut, doing a space walk is the ultimate dream. I was not disappointed, and spacewalking was the highlight of my final full month aboard the Russian space station *Mir*. Opening the door and journeying outside the space station added risk to an already risky endeavor. I was living dangerously in space.

April Fool!

Dear John,

Things are just rotten up here.

Looking out the window is boring. The same oceans and continents, day after day. As for the stars, there are just too many of them. Who can keep track? And besides, that comet Halle-Bopp is putting out so much light that it makes it difficult to see Cassiopeia.

Yesterday, the people in Mission Control–Moscow decided that three months is enough time to be in space and that I will be returning to Earth in the *Soyuz* capsule next weekend. We will just leave the space station empty until the shuttle crew arrives. Then, the whole shuttle crew will stay aboard for six months, each of them working day and night, nonstop, in order to try to do all of the experiments that were originally planned for me to do over the next two months.

Then, when I arrive on Earth, NASA plans to send me to a Caribbean island for a year or two just to relax.

John, Mom may try to fool you by saying things such as, "John, you don't have to take a nap today," or "I am sending you to Siberia." Do not fall for it. Today is April 1st, better known as April Fool's Day. Beware!

Good night. I do not miss you at all.

Dad

Up Here, You Either Make It, Bring It, or Do without It

Dear John,

The knee bone is connected to the leg bone, the leg bone is connected to the anklebone, and the anklebone is connected to the foot bone.

Up here on *Mir*, we drink water. Our urine is converted back into water. The water is hydrolyzed into hydrogen and oxygen. The hydrogen, being an explosive gas, is dumped overboard into the vacuum of space. The oxygen we breathe. We exhale carbon dioxide. Carbon dioxide is scrubbed out of the air by using an absorbent filter. The filter is flushed of its built-up carbon dioxide by periodically exposing it to the vacuum of space.

When running on the treadmill, we sweat. From our skin, the moisture evaporates in order to cool our bodies. (By the way, those doggies that you are so fascinated with use their tongues as an evaporative surface in order to lose any excessive heat that they build up. Panting is their equivalent to our sweating.) The sweat evaporates into the air. This vapor, along with all the other humidity in the air, is condensed on cold coils (just the way the outside of your cold baby bottle gets wet on a hot, humid day). After the water is collected using capillary tubes, the condensate is boiled and biocide is added. We then drink the recycled water or use it to reconstitute our freeze-dried foods. Delicious!

Another water source, and a very good one, is the space shuttle. On the shuttle, we combine liquid oxygen and liquid hydrogen (stored in tanks) to produce electricity in fuel cells.

Fortunately for the space station occupants, a byproduct of that reaction is water. On non-space-station docking flights, the water is simply dumped overboard, creating a rather spectacular blizzard of white "snow" when the dump vacuum valve is opened. On *Mir* flights, we collect the water into large rubberized sacks instead and transfer the containers to the *Mir* space station to be used later by *Mir* astronauts and cosmonauts as drinking water. We prefer drinking this water over the urine water and sweat water!

These closed-loop systems are rather ingenious environmental marvels. On the other hand, because of the interconnectedness of the system, if any single link breaks down, the entire system is in jeopardy. To quote an old Navy saying: "On the strength of one link in the cable dependeth the might of the chain."

Presently, both of the hydrolysis-based primary oxygen-generating systems are stubbornly not working. We have therefore been forced to use expendable solid-fueled oxygen generators, three a day, in order to supply sufficient breathing oxygen to sustain us. Eventually the canisters will be used up, and unless we can get the primary systems working again or, if that is not possible, we get a resupply of the canisters, we will be faced with a bad situation: insufficient oxygen to sustain life and consequently a forced evacuation from the space station.

Up here, you either make it, bring it; or do without it. Someday I will show you my Crazy Clock game (if I can find it down in Grandma Linenger's basement). Drop in a marble, which rolls down the slide, which opens a gate, which bumps a different marble onto a platform that springs a dummy into a wooden bucket. Good fun. Good future astronaut training.

Good night. Daddy is presently into round two of sleeping with wires connected to my eyelashes and electrodes fastened to my scalp and on my face. Already feeling myself depleted of blood and facing another blood collection first thing in the morning, my dreams usually center on a vampire attacking me. Sometimes I find myself waking up in the middle of the night screaming, "I didn't do it!" since the electrodes all over my face and scalp make me feel as if I were being electrocuted for some devious crime. In the morning, I have to record all of my dreams (nightmares?) on a microcassette recorder. Science!

Wishing you pleasanter dreams, John. Pass along a kiss to Mommy for me, please.

Love,
Dad

Icy Glaciers

Dear John,

Mommy wrote me a great letter filled with descriptions of how you are getting along.

You have a new word. Caa-Caa. It is unimportant that these sounds have no meaning in either Russian or English. What is important is that you know what you are trying to say. Keep practicing. Some day you might randomly make a sound that is meaningful to everyone listening. Then you will really be a hit.

I heard that you have been on vacation and running around without a snowsuit. It sure is nice to take a break from winter, isn't it?

In America, the same "flight from winter" occurs. There is a great migration to the South. If someone from Michigan, in January, ever asks you the question, "Guess where Karen just got back from?" guess Florida.

If it's phrased as a multiple choice question, with choices (a) the Hudson Bay, (b) Alaska, (c) the space station *Mir*, or (d) Florida, try to bet them a million dollars that you can guess correctly before you correctly guess "(d) Florida"!

No one has been to the Hudson Bay since Mr. Hudson. Think of Alaska and you think of icy glaciers. That is precisely what Michiganians do not want to think about in January. Few venture into space.

Put the winnings in your piggy bank. It might cover part of your college education someday. Maybe.

If you want to get away from the hustle and bustle, all coasts are to be avoided. At night, from space, the coastlines are distinct. City lights abound. Long Island lights up like a torch, as does the entire eastern seaboard. It is likewise glowing brightly along the Atlantic coast of Europe and surrounding the entire Pacific Basin. Include the inland lakes and seas—the Great Lakes, the Mediterranean, and the Black Sea—and one sees 90 percent of the nighttime lights of planet Earth. Around the planet Earthlings congregate near water.

Up here it is always quiet. Three human beings. A few lights turned on. One space station, rather insignificant in all the vastness of space. There is lots of room for more rocket-ships, space stations, outposts, and people.

Good night, John. Caa-Caa.

Love,
Dad

4 April 1997

Eight Thousand Stars

Dear John,

A person can see about eight thousand stars with the naked eye when viewing the heavens from Earth. About four thousand if you live in the Southern Hemisphere, and a slightly different set of four thousand if you live in the Northern Hemisphere. Of course, viewers can only see half of these at a time because of their set observation position on the Earth and

126

because of the interference caused by the light of day. Taking these factors into consideration, on a given night a stargazer might see about two thousand stars.

Up here I can see almost all of the stars over a very short period of time.

I have learned a new way to view them. Unattached, unthinking, and just gazing out the window, trancelike. I do not try to categorize, name, or pick out constellations. Instead, I just look.

At first I used my binoculars. But then I said to myself, "Is not eight thousand sufficient?" Sure, there are hundreds of billions of stars in our Milky Way galaxy alone and I will not see them all. So be it.

The catalogs now list over ten million stars. I am glad to know that fact, because now I can just relax when viewing the sky. No one can remember ten million of anything, right? It seems to me that perhaps, at times, we humans spend far too much time intellectualizing and thinking and too little time simply sitting back and enjoying the wonders of our world.

Last night I made my way to the window in an attempt to see the space shuttle launch from Florida. I figured that during the eight minutes of burn, I would have a fair chance of being able to see rocket engines spewing out their telltale flames. Unfortunately, I didn't see a thing, mainly because, at the time, we were atop Asia. But while looking out the window, I did make fortuitous back-to-back sightings of moving objects.

As I was looking directly to the north, above the dancing Northern Lights, I saw a very fast moving light above the horizon coming toward me and then suddenly disappearing. Then three minutes later, I saw another lit object, on a nearly identical trajectory.

What I *think* I saw were two very high altitude polar-orbiting satellites. The satellites were still catching the rays of the Sun, while Earth below was already in darkness. The satellites, if indeed that is what they were, were really moving along quickly.

John, after I land, we will set up a tent in the backyard and have a father-son camp-out. We'll look up at the stars, relax, and just enjoy being together again.

Be good. Give Mommy a smile and a kiss for me, please.

Love,
Dad

5 April 1997

Typical Father

Dear John,

Another busy, busy day today. I know that it is Saturday, but that does not count up here. Although it is almost bedtime, I am still waiting for some data to download. After that, I need to take my temperature, answer a mood questionnaire, and then put on electrodes for the sleep study.

The sleep experiment requires that I take my temperature and answer a mood-measuring questionnaire five times a day. Since the investigators are interested in how my biorhythms may have changed without the usual twenty-four-hour day-night cycles, body temperature is an important measure. Body temperature normally fluctuates throughout the day, changing in a set pattern. As far as mood, my mood is usually pretty good throughout the day until, for the fifth time in one day, I have to answer the same questions! Following the question-naire, I then put on the night headband garb—electrodes and wires over my eyelids and head—before finally heading off to my wall (bed, that is!) for sleep. This is literally working twenty-four hours a day.

I was bragging about you today over dinner. Typical father. Someone commented that by the time I get back, you will be walking. Walking, nothing! You were doing that before I left, I told them. Talking, or maybe even running, right? Right.

I knew I should not have spoken of Florida the other day. Right after that, one of the coolant loops on *Mir* sprang a leak. We had to shut it down, which means that two of the modules are now at ninety-two degrees plus. In addition, the condenser whose function it is to remove the humidity from the air uses this same coolant loop. The result is Florida-in-the-summer hot and humid "weather" up here. I suppose that this situation will help me become acclimatized and ready for the Houston summer upon landing. How is that for an optimistic outlook?

Have a good night's sleep, John. I'll be watching over you.

Love,
Dad

Earliest Memories

Dear John,

I was thinking of you and wondering how much of all of this you will someday be able to recall. The earliest event in my life that I can recall with certainty and match a date to the memory is an incident involving my Grandpa (your Great-Grandfather) Linenger. It probably occurred around 1957, putting me at the age of two. Since he died shortly thereafter, the time frame is not arguable.

I am sure that I have earlier memories, but they lack a concrete reference point in time to fix their date. In your case, the recall of events with a fixation of date might be easier to do. For example, if you remember someone standing in snow over his head, the place was Russia, and you were less than a year and a half old.

My life was different. I was born and raised in the same house. In fact, your Grandma Linenger still lives in that house. We traveled from Detroit to Chicago every year for vacation to visit our grandparents. Dad built a special wooden platform that covered the place where one would normally put one's feet in the back seat of the red Ford Fairlane 500. This contraption converted the big finned Fairlane into a sleeping den for us little ones. Mom and Dad would carry all five of us Linenger kids out to the car, asleep, in the middle of the night, placing each of us side-by-side onto our makeshift bed. And off we drove.

By the time we woke up, we were in Paw Paw, Michigan, with Chicago not far off. Dad would blow the horn to announce our arrival in Indiana, and we would all let out a cheer when seeing the Welcome to Illinois sign. We played car bingo until all of our cards were filled totally, with the exception of the S-curve sign box. Freeways were not built with S-curves and we could never convince Dad to exit the freeway and drive down some country roads in order to find an S-curve sign. When we spotted the billboard with the lips of the Magikist cleaners on it, we knew that we would be at Grandma and Grandpa's in less than "one cartoon." (Our childhood clock was not made up of hours and minutes; rather, it was calculated according to how long it took to watch one Popeye cartoon.) Hires root beer and Lays potato chips would await us at Grandma and Grandpa's home.

So you see, my early life was somewhat repetitive and nicely stable. The reason I remember the event with Grandpa Linenger is because he scolded my older brother Kenny for something and kicked him out of the new addition to our house that we were building at the time, but he let me stay. I felt lucky . . . preferential treatment. In retrospect, he probably either did not see me or did not think that I was old enough to understand words yet, so he just ignored me. In any case, I distinctly remember standing among the two-by-fours in the partially framed-in kitchen and looking up at him.

If your recall turns out to be not a lot better than mine is, at least you will have a copy of these letters. Mommy is collecting them all for you. Someday you will be able to pull them out, see what Daddy was up to, and know that I was thinking of you each and every day. There is nothing more important to Mommy and me, on Earth or in space, than you, John.

Good night. Love and miss you.

Dad

This is one of the ops reports that I sent to NASA management. It is included to illustrate the seriousness of the situation on board in order that you might better understand the circumstances under which the letters to John were written.

Operations Report

Fm.: CAPT J. M. Linenger, MC, USN
Subj.: *Mir* update.

1. I have made it a point to evaluate myself periodically throughout this flight. I have adjusted well, continue to adjust well, and continue to work efficiently. I am doing fine mentally and physically. Furthermore, I have full confidence in the present crew.

2. In the face of recent problems onboard *Mir* and the shuttle, I want to reiterate what I said before the flight: There is no need for heroics to get me back on a given vehicle at a given time. I am committed to this flight, I have been dealing with problems as they arise, and I am prepared to face any further contingencies.

3. I am, however, becoming concerned for the well-being of follow-on long-duration crew and, to a lesser extent, the shuttle crew during the docked phase. In my case, we have limited options; in their case, choices.

4. My biggest concern is the multiplicity of failures—not any single failure—and the unexplained nature of the causes in many cases (or, simply that the equipment was worn out; for example, the frayed wire that broke when I was using the treadmill). We have worked around some of these problems, but the margin seems very small indeed. The recent *Progress* docking helped to buy some more time, but does not correct all the difficulties.

Problems include cooling-loop leaks and shutdown, failed gyrodynes, fire, inability to perform physical fitness counter-measures due to high carbon dioxide levels, high temperature, total power outages in *Priroda* with no master alarm sounding, two nonfunctioning *Electron* oxygen-generating units, long-term exposure to ethylene glycol, and an unsuccessful attempt at a manual *Progress* docking with no visual information on the monitor.

5. I am not writing to get reassurances or explanations. I trust that this is being looked at carefully on the ground and that the right decisions will be made. I just wanted to emphasize that whatever the "right" decision is, I am ready to comply.

Very respectfully,
Jerry M. Linenger

Never Look at Lasers

Dear John,

I received a note the other day from my former high school swimming coach, Dave Clark. He is not the bandstand guy (his name was Dick Clark), nor is he part of the Dave Clark Five rock group that no one really cared for because they merely copied the beloved Beatles. Coach Clark was a teacher at East Detroit High School.

He wrote that people were pulling for me, thinking of me, worry over me, and proud of me back on planet Earth. That comment made me feel good inside and I worked even harder than usual today. Perhaps the sound of his name evoked a potential across a memory nerve inside my head, activating my recall of the sound of his whistle blaring and of him yelling, "Pick it up, sprint, no breathing, go!" He always pushed us hardest when our arms already felt like lead and our lungs were about to burst. Although not pleasant at the time, his prodding taught me the lesson that no matter how tired I become, no matter how much I think that I have reached my limit, it is still possible to reach down even further inside and find more energy—to tap into some hidden reserve and persist. It was a valuable lesson.

He also spoke of family, how all parents feel the same way that I do, with an almost magical love of their children.

Mommy says that you are a smart little guy. I, of course, agree. But what parent doesn't feel that about his or her child? While all children are special, our own children, when viewed

134

through the lens of parental eyes, become extra extra special. I hope that you feel secure knowing that, to Mommy and me, you are the most important, loved person in the world. An extension of the love that we have for each other.

Wow! How is that for Dad showing his soft side?

In the space business, it has once again been a busy day. Measuring diffusion coefficients in metals. Tracking my bio-rhythms. Recording radiation levels. Examining microbes on petri dishes. Checking crew health. Looking ahead and reviewing contingency procedures for the planned *Progress* resupply vehicle docking tomorrow.

In spite of the heavy workload, I did find time to glance out the window as we passed over the Amazon. Sadly, I saw smoke plume after smoke plume rising into the atmosphere from fires burning below. The fires are being intentionally lighted in order to clear-cut the jungle for farming. The people on the ground probably do not realize the extent of the damage that they're causing. The view from space makes it all too clear.

Japan at night was once again spectacular. The entire coastline was aglow from the lights of towns and cities, with Tokyo shining as brightly and over as wide an area as any city on Earth.

One place that I will not be looking down at is France. They will be conducting a tracking experiment tonight, attempting to aim a laser at us as we zoom by them. It is wise not to put one's retina in the path of a laser beam. There is a new one to add to your list of do's and don'ts, John. Right after "Don't bite other people's legs," add "Never look at lasers out the windows of spacecraft." I know that it must be difficult keeping track of all these do's and don'ts!

I hope that you had another adventurous learning day yourself, John. Good night. Pleasant dreams. Love you.

Dad

Progress Resupply Spacecraft Docking

Dear John,

I heard that you cried "appropriately, but not too much," during your last set of immunizations. That completes the set—no more needed before you go to school. Now you can relax, because school is still a long way off.

We had a flawless docking of our *Progress* resupply spacecraft yesterday. The *Progress* brought up a lot of items: repair kits, carbon dioxide absorber canisters, oxygen canisters, and other needed equipment. The vehicle was unmanned and was docked in the automatic mode.

Let me describe what the docking looked like from my vantage inside the space station.

I first spotted the spacecraft when I was looking out of a window to port. I could make out the solar panels of the *Progress*, which were properly aligned perpendicular to the rays of the Sun in order to capture as much solar energy as possible. The solar panels of *Progress* matched the orientation our space station solar panels precisely. When first seen, the spacecraft was bathed in brilliant light. Because of its altitude, the Sun was lighting it up, while below the spacecraft, Earth was still in darkness.

As sunrise occurred on Earth below, I could see that we were located directly above Buenos Aires. Farther north along the coast of South America, I could see that the *Progress* vehicle was directly over Rio de Janeiro. It was difficult to ascertain which of us was flying higher, but it was clear that we were both covering the same track.

As we both flew over the Atlantic Ocean, it became apparent that we were gaining ground. Occasionally, my view became obstructed as the spacecraft dipped behind our solar panels. I was reporting to the *Mir* commander, Vasily, that I had the *Progress* clearly in sight. He would fly over to the window, take a look, and see nothing. I would look again and see the spaceship plain as day. Vasily would look again and once again report, "I don't see a thing." We finally realized that our timing was such that every time that he would look, the *Progress* would have dipped from view behind our solar panel, and when I would look again, the spacecraft was once again in plain view. I had already made a note to myself that I would have to do an eye exam on him after the docking. He was probably thinking I needed a psychological exam for "seeing things"!

By Africa, *Progress* suddenly appeared to be closing the gap between us at a very fast rate. The spacecraft was sliding toward us from port, and becoming bigger and brighter by the second. By the time we reached the Mediterranean and darkness, the *Progress* had once again settled nicely in front of us (but toward the back of the space station, since we were flying tail-first). We finally docked just to the east of the Caspian Sea.

As I watched its final approach through a small porthole two feet from where the actual station docking mechanism is located, *Progress* looked like a four-eyed monster—one low "headlight" with three smaller lights across the top. The solar panels resembled outstretched arms. The spacecraft would "blow its top" (and bottom, but never its sides) every three seconds or so as braking thrusters fired. Each time the thrusters fired, I could see snowflake-like particle debris dancing in space very near the window that I was looking out.

The docking itself produced a loud hhrruuummppphhh, followed by a second, softer hrrumpphh. The station was visibly shaken during this controlled collision. Monitors swayed, the floor moved under my feet, and the flexible pleated ventilation tubes began an accordion motion, first folding in and out strongly, then more mildly, then ever so weakly, and finally, almost imperceptibly. The motion damped out completely after these four movements.

Upon opening our hatch, I could smell "space." Space has a rather nondistinct, almost absence of smell, distantly resembling the smell of already spent logs found in a stone-cold fireplace in the morning. When I opened the second hatch, the *Progress* hatch, I was overwhelmed by the aroma of fresh fruit. The fresh apples and lemons were a special-delivery gift from our friends on Earth.

Orientation and relative motion between two bodies is difficult to discern precisely in space. The relative motion is further complicated by the spin of Earth below. It is even more difficult to describe such motion in words. When I said that *Progress* was ahead of us, I meant in flight path. But since we were flying "backwards" at the time—pointing the space station's rear docking port at the *Progress*—it was "behind" us relative to the space station. To further confound the issue, one got the best view out of the window by floating upside down relative to the floor of the module that I was in.

Picture this: driving ninety miles an hour down the freeway, in reverse, with the car flipped upside down. Instead of sitting on the seat, you are standing on your head, looking out the driver's side window. You look behind you (toward the back of the car, which is in the direction of forward travel) and see an entrance ramp up ahead. Another vehicle is entering the freeway. The merging vehicle is sliding in from the ramp so fast that you instinctively move your foot toward the brake pedal because it is difficult to ascertain whether the vehicle will "blend in" nicely ahead of your car or collide with you. After some frantic moments, the merging car does indeed find its place in front of you and continues moving at the precise speed that you are presently moving. The car in front then begins to brake every three seconds or so until you bump its headlight on the rear bumper of the car that you are traveling in. You hear and feel the collision, and the bumpers lock. Docking between the two vehicles is complete.

The above description is a pretty darned good analogy. If you can picture it, you can understand what the *Progress* docking looked and felt like and, perhaps, understand why hearts race during the merging phase between two massive and fast-moving (18,000 miles per hour) space vehicles.

If Mommy is reading this letter to you as a bedtime story, I picture your eyes closed by now, with you drifting into sweet, restful sleep. Pleasant dreams, John.

Love,
Dad

Psychological Support

Dear John,

You are not the only one whom Mommy teases occasionally.

Today I opened my "psychological support package" that had arrived on the *Progress* resupply ship yesterday. Because room is limited on the spacecraft, with important equipment and supplies taking up most of the space, Mommy had to squeeze all of my personal items into a purse-sized sack.

In it were some fantastic pictures of your handsome little self. In addition, and surprisingly, were the first "pictures"— ultrasounds—of your future sibling. On the envelope, Mommy had written, "boy or girl?" With you, she would never let the doctors tell her the sex and would never show me the ultrasounds, preferring to be surprised at the birth. I quickly opened the envelope, floated to the ceiling, held the ultrasound films up to the light and studied them. Beautiful head . . . cute little feet and arms . . . good-looking spine . . . and a well-formed heart.

But somebody snitched the all-important "distinguishing feature" film (and I bet I know who!). Without that film, it means that you and I still do not know whether you will be having a brother or a sister to play with someday. Another surprise on the way.

Getting that package has really made me happy. In it were lots of pictures of our friends, family, and relatives. Most of those photos were taken when they were down in Florida for my launch. Since I was in quarantine the whole week prior to launch and was, of course, in the shuttle during the launch, I missed the whole shebang in Cocoa Beach. But the pictures reflect that there was quite a crowd down there and that they were all having a good time.

In addition to the photos, most everyone wrote a little something about their witnessing the launch of the shuttle. Comments included: "Absolutely fantastic." "It lit up the whole sky." "What tremendous power." "I will never, ever forget the experience." "We were wondering the whole time what it must be like for you inside that thing, and shouting, 'Go, Jerry, Go!'" From their comments, it sounds as though they liked it almost as much as I did. I'm glad. To me, a shuttle launch is something that every American—heck, every human being—should witness in order to share in the overwhelming feeling of pride in what we human beings can accomplish.

It somehow makes it easier to keep pushing myself, to keep working hard, and to keep overcoming obstacles knowing that I am in people's thoughts and prayers, knowing that they are pulling for me and for the success of our mission. I give it my best.

John, I want you to know that I will always, always be pulling for you and that you will always, always be in my thoughts and prayers.

Good night, my favorite little boy in the whole wide world. You sure are a handsome little rascal when you strike your own classic pose: one hand positioned with thumb in mouth and the other hand tugging on your earlobe. That's my boy.

Dad

Sneaking Up

Dear John,

Remember that game we played, where I would peep around the corner of the sofa and try to sneak up on you? When you saw me, you would laugh and laugh.

Well, up here it is really great. No sounds of footsteps and no creaking floor. I can fly silently through the air and the unsuspecting victim has no clue that I am coming.

My sneaking up on crewmates always evokes a startled response. I can't say that they actually "jump," because usually they are already floating. But you can hear them gasp and then their arms and legs flail about. Inevitably they try to pretend that they were not startled at all, that they were *expecting* me to come flying by. Tee-hee.

Of course I do not *intentionally* try to sneak up and scare my fellow cosmonauts, but it happens quite naturally and often during the course of a day. As a matter of fact, something (someone?) just bumped into my leg. Hmmm, just a floating food container gone astray and causing my heartbeat to jump a bit.

Speaking of hearts, they have a pretty easy life up here. My blood pressure has been consistently low, especially the big number—the systolic blood pressure. Pulse fifty-ish. It is like a vacation for the heart up here, since there is no blood pooling in the legs that needs to be moved by the heart pump and no gravity to make the blood "heavy." Only my treadmill work-outs challenge the heart muscle in a meaningful way. And, of course, when someone else sneaks up unexpectedly on me.

Okay, I admit it. I do fly my approaches toward my unsus-pecting crewmates a bit closer than necessary sometimes and hold off on the urge to clear my throat. I think this aberrant behavior can be traced back to my childhood.

We were at a creaky cottage in Michigan. Just the boys, fathers and sons. The cottage was a rustic place, located in the middle of nowhere. We were playing a card game called euchre in the cottage next door to the one that we were staying in. My brother Kenny lost and went back, alone, to our cottage.

As I returned after the card game and quietly opened the door to our cottage, I found him peacefully watching a late-night movie, fully reclined, feet up, on a Lazyboy. How I got to a position directly behind him without the floor creaking to alert him, I will never know. Once in position, I remained silently behind him until the program reached a suspenseful moment, then I grabbed him solidly with both of my arms and screamed as loud as I could into his ear, "RAAA!"

Never had I, nor will I ever again see, a startled response to top his. He bolted straight up off the chair, his arms shaking wildly. Air whooshed out of his mouth, but without an accom-panying yell or scream. His adrenaline exhausted, he was too worn out afterward to beat me up—which I had fully expected from my bigger, stronger brother. He just collapsed back into the chair, gave me the dirtiest look he could muster, tried to say something but was unable to form the words, and finally stumbled off to bed fully spent. It was great. And that, I believe, is where my devious sneak-up behavior originated.

All right, it's your bedtime and mine. I have the new photo I received of you, with angel wings and a halo drawn onto it. (Now *that* is pushing it a bit. I would bet that you would try to scare your Unkie Kenny just like I did, given the opportunity.) The photo is attached to the wall across from the wall on which I sleep. Before closing my eyes each night I look at your angelic picture and think of you and Mommy. Good night to you both.

Love,
Dad

13 April 1997

Diapers Aren't So Bad

Dear John,

You sure are an active, curious little guy.

I just finished viewing a videocassette of you that Mommy sent up on the *Progress* resupply spaceship. In the span of a minute, you beeped the horn on your toy car; pushed it round the corner; ate some tangerine segments; chased after Mommy; leafed through the Where Is Spot book, opening all of the doors inside of the book; and then grabbed the microphone off the camera. With all of that energy, you would make a great astronaut someday should you decide that is what you would like to do.

I have been busy, too. As I have told you in the past, we have had quite a few breakdowns of various vital mechanical systems. Now that some of the repair parts and specially designed tools have arrived on board, we are attempting to get things up and running again. The heightened activity reminds me of the beginning of a home improvement project after a Home Depot shopping spree, with tools and gear all over the place and the space station looking very disorderly. But, hopefully, we will be able to plug the leaks (cooling lines), install the new parts (oxygen generators), and reactivate the other failed systems.

Yes, constantly replacing the oxygen in the air that we breathe is important. Scrubbing the air of carbon dioxide is vital. Supplying cooling to the mechanical equipment is absolutely necessary. But problems with the toilet, from the perspective of a crewmember needing to use the facility, jump right to the top of our "things to do" list. We have been able to make the toilet functional only by using it in the "manual mode." In this mode, the separator section (designed to convert most of the urine to water) and the urine "conserving" section (which adds chemicals to the leftover, concentrated urine to prevent microbial growth) do not work. This is obviously less than ideal and will eventually manifest itself as an insufficient supply of water on board.

As a backup waste collection system, we use small condom-fitted leak-proof sacks. During the early space program sacks such as these were the primary means of collecting human waste and are still commonly referred to as *Apollo* bags in the U.S. program. As I said, our priority is to fix the toilet. Now you might agree that wearing diapers is not so bad after all, right?

Enjoy your carefree living, John. Daddy will be home soon and we will do some relaxing together. I realize that the meaning of relaxing for me will mean chasing you around the room, throwing you balls, taking things out of your mouth, reading to you, and trying to coax you into a nap so that I can recover. But I look forward to our time together nonetheless.

Love you and miss you. Give Mommy at least a dozen kisses for me, please. Tell her that I saw on videotape a television interview that she did a while back and she did a great job. I am proud of her.

Dad

14 April 1997

Make a Snowball While You Can

Dear John,

I understand that this will be your last week living in Russia. Here is a list of things you might consider doing before leaving.

1. Make a snowball while you can.
2. Enjoy one final stroll around the pond, pointing out all of the dogs and cats in Star City.
3. Use all your Russian words now. When you get home, people will think that you are still in the babbling stage of oral development when you say zdrastvoutya. They will not understand that you are saying hello and will think that you are a bit behind other little boys your age that can already say goo rather proficiently.

4. Most important of all, give everyone one of your biggest smiles and maybe one of your kisses. Especially Vera, who has been helping Mommy and me out with you since you were a month old. She will really miss you, John, and you her. She loved you freely, helped to care for you, taught you Russian words, and was your friend. A very nice part of being in Russia for our whole family, wasn't she? We will all miss her.

Well, I had better get back to work. I finished installing the replacement fire extinguishers and I must admit that it feels good to be back at full, fire-fighting strength once again. There is still lots more to do, but I just wanted you and Mommy to know that I was thinking about you, love you, and really miss you both.

Dad

15 April 1997

Speed Equates to Altitude

Dear John,

We are a bit farther apart today than we were yesterday.

While space is essentially a vacuum, it is not a perfect vacuum. We do slow down over time due to particle friction. When you strike an object while moving at 18,000 miles per hour, no matter how small the particle, there is a reaction to it and the *Mir* slows. This is similar to when you pedal your bicycle: stop pedaling, and sooner or later, you will slow to a stop.

Speed equates to altitude when you are in orbit. We go faster in order to get up higher. As we slow down, our orbit lowers. The lower the *Mir* sinks, the more particles and remnants of Earth's atmosphere we run into and we begin to slow at an even a greater rate. If we decelerate too much, we will reenter the atmosphere. The atmosphere is so thick with particles that friction dominates and the whole spaceship really heats up. Without proper protection, the spacecraft will burn up. Since *Mir* is not equipped with heat-protection tiles, there is no way to safely de-orbit the space station.

In a month or so, I obviously *want* to reenter and to land once again on planet Earth. In order to do that, I will have to switch vehicles and ride home on board the shuttle. We will fire thrusters to slow us down and then use the thick atmosphere to slow us still further. During reentry, it is crucial to keep the heat-protective tiles pointed in the proper direction. On board, we will see a fireball engulf us and hear loud booms. In fact, the sound of reentry resembles that of a runaway locomotive trying to run us down from behind.

But going home will have to wait. Since space stations are designed to live in space permanently, every so often we have to speed up in order to raise our altitude. That is what we did today.

Using a single large thruster and unspent fuel from the *Progress* resupply vehicle that docked with us last week, we did a "burn" of about two minutes. The burn was very gradual and we accelerated very gently. Although the sensation felt inside the station was much gentler than the boom-slam you feel on shuttle when firing its thrusters, the motion was still discernible, especially after a hundred days of quiet.

I positioned myself at the farthest point in one of the branching modules in order to maximize the sensation. Although I had already activated some very sensitive sensors to detect the acceleration and any bending moments imparted to the space station modules themselves (the data to be used when designing future space complexes), I wanted to *feel* it with my human sensors. It was nighttime on Earth below and I could see the light flashes from the firing thruster. When I let go of the handhold, I would immediately float toward the "ceiling." This acceleration force was apparent throughout the two-minute burn. Not a strong force, but definite. At cutoff, I could feel the whole module gently swaying in response, four or five times, before settling. Two minutes or so later, I saw more light flashes from multiple thruster firings, this time a bit brighter. I suspect that these were smaller space station thruster firings used to turn the whole station into the correct orientation relative to the Sun. By the way, all of this positioning of *Mir* was done via signals from the ground; in fact, the *Mir* commander was eating lunch at the time.

The result is that I am now flying higher and that you are farther away. But you and Mommy are still close in my thoughts, and soon we will be close enough to hold onto one another.

Pleasant dreams. Love you.

Dad

Making the Door

Dear John,

It looks like my good friend Mark Clark is moving back to St. Louis from Michigan. I am sure that he is not pleased. But you sometimes have to go places where work takes you. (I should know, right?)

When we first met back at the Naval Academy at Annapolis, Maryland, over twenty years ago, I told Mark that I was from Michigan. His response was "Ooohhhaaahhh. I love Michigan!" Although he was from St. Louis, it seems that his family from way back (grandparents) had a cottage in Saugatuck, Michigan, where they would spend their summers. He spent a part of almost every summer of his life along the shores of Lake Michigan—walking the beach, swimming, hiking through the woods, taking dune buggy rides, canoeing—all of those great doings of summer.

Their cottage has character. Built on top of a sand dune with woods surrounding, it has a big back porch and knotty pine paneling inside. You sleep with the window cracked open on old, creaky beds to the sound of the waves, with blankets piled high and covers pulled to the tip of your nose, breathing in the fresh air. Showers were taken in the lake with bar of soap in hand.

My goal at this whimsical place was to make it on a door. Let me explain.

Every door in the cottage had six or eight panes. At the close of the summer, the family would paint the year at the top

150

of one of the panes, reminisce a bit about the happenings of the year, and then paint simple little pictures with captions to highlight those events. The year 1954 might have a picture of a chunky baby with squinty eyes with the accompanying caption "Mark born," maybe a sketch of a tipped canoe, a new flagpole raised, and perhaps a storm cloud over Lake Michigan.

The years add up and by now practically every door in the cottage is painted with treasured memories of years past.

I think I first made an appearance on a door in 1977 when, after graduation from Annapolis, Mark and a few of his friends spent a week at the cottage. The sketch showed a gang of gung-ho Popeyes dressed in sailor caps with the caption "New Ensigns Arrive." I made a door again in 1990 when I asked Mommy to marry me when we were at Saugatuck and she said yes. The sketch was of a sparkling diamond ring. And most recently my mug was on the door in 1994 with the caption "Liftoff" and a sketch of the space shuttle *Discovery*.

When you look at those doors, three things of importance immediately hit you. Time marches on, family endures, and people will not be around forever.

We, as a family, are going to find a door and start sketching. Your birthday will make the 1995 door pane, a snowflake representing our time together in Russia on the 1996 door, and your sibling-to-be on the 1997 door. And maybe the Halle-Bopp comet with me riding it and Mommy holding down the fort. Family endures.

Good night. Love you. A kiss to Mommy, please.

Dad

151

We Are Two Lucky Men

Dear John,

We sure did surprise Mommy, didn't we? From up here, it sounded like quite a gang was gathered at her "going away from Russia" farewell party. I was glad that Mission Control–Moscow was able to patch me through on radio to talk with her and to add to her surprise.

In case you could not hear what I said, here is a recap. Kathryn, you are the most wonderful wife in the world. There are not a lot of women who would move to Russia for almost two years, raise our newborn there, be expecting again, and have her husband not only leave, but *leave the planet* for months at a time. Throughout it all you have been supportive, understanding, cheerful, and positive. And in the midst of all of those demands, you have done a fantastic job in training cosmonauts and astronauts for the medical science portion of their flights to *Mir*. I love you. I miss you. And I can't wait to be together again.

From the sounds that I could make out in the background, a lot of other people agree with me.

John, you are blessed with a great mommy and I with a great wife. We are two lucky men.

Have a safe journey home. I will see you both back in the USA in a month or so after the shuttle lands. Can't wait!

Love,
Dad

I Sleep Soundly at Night

Dear John,

During a radio interview yesterday, they surprised me and had your Grandma Linenger on to say hello. She greeted me, told me that everyone was thinking about me, and then said that she can't wait until I get home safe and sound. She sounded a bit worried.

The interviewer asked if I was worried, too. I answered honestly, no, and told her that I sleep soundly at night. She observed that I sure sounded nice and calm.

The difference between my mother worrying and me remaining calm, I think, is one of control. Undoubtedly, orbiting at 18,000 miles per hour in a vacuum, being dependent on life support systems for pressure, oxygen, and carbon dioxide removal, and facing multiple breakdowns of those vital systems is just cause for worry. But at the same time, I know the hazards. I have prepared myself to face them through training and study, and I now have the real-life experience of having overcome problems through my own actions. I stay concerned, yes. I think about possible contingencies and how we, the crew, would respond. But I do not *worry* about something that is out of my control and might not happen anyway.

On the other hand, I do worry about you and Mommy— about your health, your safety when traveling, and even the possibility of you falling down the stairs! I am out here in space and have no control over what happens down there.

My mother was worried about me. She, of course, can do nothing to intervene in my problems; she can do nothing to

153

help me. Plus, worrying is just part of the nature of our mothers, right? We are all fortunate to have them thinking about us our whole lives long.

I snapped a photo of Athens, Greece, today. I used the biggest lens that I could find in order to try to spot you and Mommy on the ground. I saw clearly the harbor and some major roads (railroads?) leading from the city—but no Johnchek, no Mommy. I was just trying to keep an eye on you two. I saw that the weather was nice down there for your arrival. When I return, we will have to compare photos: Mommy's up-close views of Athens and my distant space shots.

Happy travels. I'll be watching over you and worrying about you.

Love,
Dad

19 April 1997

Seeing It All

Dear John,

I continue to be surprised every time that I look down on Earth. I thought that after a hundred days in space I would have seen it all, but that is just not the case.

Today, looking at fish-shaped Sakhalin Island, the Kamchatka Peninsula, and the Kuril Islands almost took my breath away. (All of these sites are north of the island of Hokkaido, Japan.)

Splintering ice flows surrounded Sakhalin—huge flows thrust up on each other. Farther out to sea, I could see graceful windmill-like swirls of solid white ice against the deep blue sea. Someone on a ship amidst the melting ice would not see or appreciate the delicate swirling pattern that the flow paints over a hundred miles or so of ocean.

Kamchatka looked as if it belonged on a different planet: ragged peaks and volcanic domes, one after another. Brilliant white in the snow.

The Kuril Islands were under cloud cover—almost. I could only see a single peak from each island poking out above the cirrus cloud layer. The peaks were spaced out a hundred miles or so, but you could site right down the tube and see that they made an almost perfectly straight line. One hot spot had erupted through a weakness in Earth's crust, and the lava that flowed to the surface had formed these islands. The hot lava was cooled by the ocean and formed the lone island peaks. Subsequent movement of Earth's crust eventually moved the weakened area of the crust away from the hot spot, and new crust closed off the leak of lava to the surface temporarily. This movement of Earth's crust at the same time changed the location of the newly created island, which, of course, sits on the crust. Thousands of years later, another weak spot in Earth's crust arrived over the same hot spot, another eruption resulted, and another island was created. One after another. It was remarkable for me to witness the end result of million of years of geological activity—a string of islands stretching south to north.

There is nothing so rewarding as learning, discovering new things. I saw it in your face every day, John. For example, I can still picture the big smile that came to your face when you finally figured out that the cross-shaped block fit perfectly into the cross-shaped hole in the box. You repeated the action, and sure enough, it worked the second time. You were one happy boy.

That feeling never goes away. The pure delight of learning, of discovery. There is so much out there that we will never become bored. Life is a joy.

I hope that you are exploring something new today, John, and that you have another big smile on your face. Good night. Sweet and interesting dreams.

Dad

PS: You know, now that I think about it, I wonder what an eighteen-month-old dreams about. I know that children "sleep deep" and that with age we get less and less deep sleep and more and more of the light, dreaming variety of sleep: REM (rapid eye movement) sleep. But surely, you have your own unique dreams also.

20 April 1997

My New World

Dear John,

I have a picture of you taped to the wall in front of my work area. Your face wears a mischievous smirk, the kind of look that alerts me immediately that you are up to something and that I had better keep my eye on you. I love that picture. I love that look on your face. It shows that you are raring to go try something new.

Living in space has been something new for me. The strangeness of the environment has worn off gradually. It is now to the point that floating, flying, and living in a confined space without seeing new faces and without having real days or real nights seem normal. This is my new world.

Today, I talked to my friends Cousin Tom Linenger and Jim Brant during my once-a-week family call to Earth. They mentioned that they were looking for a fourth to go golfing with today and invited me. I declined since I was never much of a golfer anyway and it was too inconvenient to travel from space to the course. I suggested that they ask you, figuring that if you start early enough you might play like Tiger Woods someday and we could all retire. We then talked of old times, of my upcoming space walk, and of getting together somewhere in Michigan after I land for a reunion of sorts. I could have talked all day.

This is my world now and I accept it fully. I try to take advantage of its uniqueness, try to keep my spirits up, and try to carry on day after day. I know that I am doing something that counts, something that matters, and something that is bigger than me as a person. I know that the risks taken and personal sacrifices are worth it.

But after that conversation, I also realized how extraordinary and wonderful life on Earth really is. One can choose to go golfing should one be in the mood for frustration. Or simply sit and read the newspaper under a big shade tree. Or spend time in the garden. A myriad of choices is always available.

Conversations without purpose can be entered into and one can talk for as long as one pleases. The conversation does not have to be about data results or about operational procedures, but rather, spontaneous and carefree talk. On Earth, one can spend time with friends and share meals together. Go outside and breathe in the fresh air. Be with family, be with you, and be with Mommy.

I will never take the simple beauty of Earth and all that it offers for granted again. I will appreciate quiet nights, calmness, swaying trees, ice cubes, carefree days, and being together. Living on an outpost, being isolated and far from Earth, has taught me this lesson.

Good night, John. Love and miss both you and Mommy. Pleasant dreams.

Dad

21 April 1997

One Hundred Days in Space

Dear John,

I just completed one hundred days in space.

I still recall vividly how you looked the last time that I saw you, one hundred and three days ago.

You were sitting in your carseat, reaching out for me to release you, grab you, and hold you; but I was in quarantine and could only look at you through the window. Mommy and you drove away. It was a gloomy day. I stood there alone and thought, "Man, am I going to miss that little guy." I was right.

Good night. I love and miss you a lot.

Dad

Doctoring Myself

Dear John,

There's that good looking number 22 again. Another month must have passed.

Today I am busy moving old, worn space suits out of the airlock and replacing them with the new ones. We are preparing to go outside for a walk next week.

Getting prepared and ready for a space walk is not as simple as you might imagine. We need to verify that all of the systems work properly—the airlock itself, the space suits, and the science equipment that we will be taking out and mounting on the exterior of the space station. Furthermore, the people on the ground want to verify that Vasily and I are healthy enough and strong enough to do the work, which means we will be doing lots of EKGs, exercise endurance tests, blood tests, and onboard physical exams.

With me being the only physician on board, I do all of the physical exams, including my own. To be honest, when doing my own exam, I always know what I will conclude before I even start the exam. This is because I have been keeping pretty good tabs on my health since arriving up here and I know how I have been feeling lately. As far as the exam to determine whether I am fit to do the space walk, I would have to be dead before I would disqualify myself for that opportunity. I wrote the result section of the progress note before the exam: Normal examination–passed.

159

I worked backward from there. Using a mirror to look at my eyes and throat, I then wrote, "Nonerythematous, no exudates noted." As a physician, I have learned that one must use those kinds of big words or people will not believe that you know what you are doing! I felt for nodes, listened through the stethoscope to my heart and lungs, and noted, "No murmurs, chest clear to rales and rhonchi." I then cleared my ears, and although I could not devise a method to actually see my eardrums move, I could feel them functioning properly. I recorded, "Positive Valsalva." I knew that my arms and legs were working just fine because I had just finished running on the treadmill prior to the exam. My reflexes were, if anything, hyperactive, but I assumed that they appeared so because there was no weight resistance to their action. I made the annotation: "Extremities, full range of motion, reflexes strong and intact." My blood pressure and pulse were low, but normal for being in space, and my oral temperature was within normal limits.

Conclusion: Normal exam. I knew it! I was ready to go spacewalking. I then scribbled my nearly illegible doctor-looking signature to the bottom of page of the progress note.

I hope that you feel fine, too, John. I heard that Mommy caught a "going-away-from-Russia" cold. I hope that you avoided catching it and that she is getting back to normal. Up here, you can only catch things from two other people, and since we all started disease-free and quarantined for a week before the flight, we have generally remained healthy.

Pleasant dreams. Back to work for me. Hold the kiss until Mommy's cold is gone, but please give her a big smile for me. Thanks.

Love,
Dad

You Overcome and Endure

Dear John,

I talked with two ABC Radio Network stations today. Both interviews focused on the technical difficulties we have had, and continue to experience, on board *Mir*. For half a minute, they could not hear me, but I could still hear them. They filled the time by listing the difficulties that I have encountered over my stay on the space station, and commented that "he sure has overcome things and endured."

Space exploration and space colonization in its infancy is a tough enterprise. We rely on machines to provide the essentials of life. We are isolated, almost completely, and therefore need to be self-sufficient to a degree that is hard to comprehend. We are surrounded by vacuum and are traveling at a screeching 18,000 miles per hour. Almost every piece of equipment is vital. There is no room for mistakes. I conduct complex experiments in dozens of disciplines and am responsible for executing them properly. Our survival depends upon doing things correctly not once, but every time.

In spite of this pressure to perform, we do indeed overcome and endure.

Undoubtedly, we are able to overcome the difficulties because we believe in what we are doing. That the work counts for something. That the struggle is worth our personal sacrifices.

I have prepared myself by training hard and studying hard. I anticipated that living and working on *Mir* was going to be tough going. I was not totally surprised when it turned out that way.

The interviewer closed the show by saying, "Well, you sure sound good." I thanked them and told them that I feel good, that it was a privilege to be representing them up here, and that I am looking forward to the month ahead on board the space station. One must reach deep and rise above the circumstances.

Good night, sleep tight. Love you.

Dad

24 April 1997

Heavy Eyes

Dear John,

I hope that your eyes feel as heavy as mine do, and that you will sleep solidly the whole night long. I am quite sure that Mommy would like that, too.

Love you. Give Mommy a kiss and a smile for me, please. I will try to find time tomorrow to write you a real letter.

Dad

Wearing a Russian Space Suit

Dear John,

I spent the day preparing and testing out the space suit that I will be using to do the space walk next week. The preparation was not unlike getting you ready for your daily walk in Russia during the winter.

To prepare you for your walks, first I had to stabilize you in order to keep you from squirming and sliding away while I put a fresh diaper on you. For some reason, you preferred being naked, and while you were cooperative during the undressing part, you always showed strength and fight beyond your months whenever I tried to put a new diaper on you.

In order to get dressed up here, I have to first stabilize both my equipment and myself. I hold on to handholds and care-fully arrange my gear behind bungee cords that are attached to the bulkheads. We start with underwear, an EKG monitor, a one-piece lightweight cotton coverall with pass-through holes to accommodate the EKG cables, and heavy socks. The heavy socks are important because open space resembles Russian winter: bitter cold when traveling on the dark side of Earth. A heat sensor used to monitor my body temperature is attached behind my ear. I slide into the coverall while floating, using handholds to stabilize myself.

The next step for you was to start putting on your layers of clothing. You were always a moving target. All of your clothes were cursed with snaps. It seemed as if no matter how carefully I aligned those snaps, I would always end up with an unmatched snap at the end and be forced to start the process over again. After two or three tries and still no success, I would admit defeat, and proclaim the closure of the outfit to be "good enough." I would then move on to the next step: inserting you into the one-piece coat-and-pants outfit that looked more like a bag than a coat.

After stuffing you into this bag-coat, I would then put on your Michigan State University beanie hat. The hat was compliments of your Aunt Susan, of course. I would then pull the hooded part of the bag-coat over the top of the beanie hat in an attempt to cover up the green Spartan. By this point you were inevitably crying and struggling to get your hands and feet free from the confining outfit.

Then the inspector would show up. Her name was Mommy. What, no socks? I would argue in vain that it was not that cold out. She would give me a stern look that suggested that she thought that I was crazy. (Well, minus twenty is warmer than minus thirty, right? And besides, who wants to do those darn snaps again with you screaming at the top of your lungs.). She would dress you again, get the snaps right in a snap, hoist you into my backpack, and we would (finally!) be off.

Up here, I wiggle into a second layer of clothing: a full-body garment laced with water tubes weaving their way through the elastic cloth. The tubes are sewn into the inner garment in order to provide for cooling. The Russian version has an attached hood that also contains the water tubes. Space-walking is hard physical work. In order to avoid becoming dehydrated or hyperthermic, the walker needs to get rid of the metabolic heat that he or she generates. Furthermore, if one becomes too hot inside the suit, there is a good chance that the visor will fog up. Not being able to see through the visor would not be good, given that we move along the surface of the space station by attaching, detaching, and reattaching two tethers along handrails. Moving in such a manner is difficult even under the best of circumstances, but it would be nearly impossible if one were, in effect, blindfolded. A ventilator (fan) and a moisture collector also help to combat this potential problem of fogging in the space suit.

On top of the cooling garment we put another hat—a communications cap—that makes me look like Rocky the Squirrel. I then crawl into the bulky space suit through a backdoor opening. The space suit on Earth weighs more than I weigh myself. Up here it floats. It is nevertheless confining and, being under pressure in order to protect the occupant from the vacuum of space, extremely bulky. Once in the suit, I am transformed into a self-contained spacecraft.

After both Vasily and I are fully suited, we check each other out and then the ground checks us out via telemetry. No snaps can be left undone. Mommy would be good at this part of the operation.

Back in Russia, once you and I went out the door, you would quit crying immediately and thoroughly enjoy the walk. You especially enjoyed pulling my hat off and I would be forced to concede that Mommy was right about it being cold outside as my then unprotected ears became nearly instantly frostbitten.

I think that all of my preparation will pay off. Not just the recent preparation up here in space, but also all the long hours spent on the ground training underwater in the training tank wearing space suit mockups. Once I open the hatch, I will start smiling broadly, just like you used to smile during your walks, John. Good night. Pleasant dreams.

Love,
Dad

Forgiveness for Times Not Spent Together

Dear John,

Whenever people get a television camera stuck in their face unexpectedly, they invariably say, "Hi, Mom." Why not half the time, "Hi, Dad," or better yet, "Hi, Mom, hi, Dad"?

I love the heck out of you, John. A deeply felt father's love for his son. There is nothing unique about it. I would suspect that all fathers feel the same sort of love for their own children. But that does not take away from its depth, sincerity, or unbending nature. I would do anything for you.

Yet I have been away from you since January, haven't I? I am told that when you see my picture, you point and say, "Mommy." You have not learned the word "Daddy" yet. That is my fault.

All of us fathers need to do better. We need to openly show our love to our children. We need to connect with them, spend time with them, and guide them. Mothers are not substitutes for fathers. We fathers should not sit back and think to ourselves, "She sure is doing a great job with the kids," or, "I could

166

never be that good at raising the children myself, so I will just stay out of the way." I believe that our sons and daughters will forgive us if their shirt is put on backwards or one snap is left undone, but they will hardly remember us at all if we are not there to hold them and to encourage them.

I have a pretty good excuse this time for not being with you. But us fathers are pretty good at excuses. We are too busy with work, too tired, too interested in the football game on television. We need to work on the computer or we have to meet with friends after work. You name it—we have all the excuses. Our priorities are often not ordered in the way that they need to be arranged.

So instead of making the excuse "I was in space," let me instead just ask your forgiveness for times not spent together. And while I am at it, Mommy's too.

Love and miss you both.

Dad

27 April 1997
Letter A

Cabin Fever

Dear John,
It is evening and tonight I feel like doing something, going somewhere.

But there is nowhere to go. I am trapped, a captive. No new faces to look at, no Mommy to talk to, no you to hold.

A simple walk would be fine. Or perhaps a paddle in the canoe. Doing something indoors just will not meet my needs. I need fresh air. I need to feel a breeze. I need to be moving freely in open and unconfined spaces.

Camping would be good. You and Mommy and me sitting under the stars by a campfire or perhaps lying in our tent. Telling stories beside a flickering lantern. The campfire casting dancing shadows on the surrounding trees. Wrestling with you. Watching you pound your head up and down on the pillow. Oh, yes, we would cheat and take big feather pillows in addition to the sleeping bags. Mommy and I would try to keep you from crawling toward our feet and biting our toes. I can almost hear the wind rustling through the trees overhead.

Since Mommy is about due to deliver you a brother or a sister, maybe camping is not such a good idea. How about just sitting on Grandma Linenger's front porch in the neighborhood that I grew up. Waving to Harold and Bernice and Glen and Shirley as they relax on their front porches. Everything so very familiar, normal, and pleasantly reassuring. We could watch it get dark and listen to the crickets chirping. As the night air grows chilly, we can cover up our legs with one of the comforters that your Great-Grandma Pusavc made by hand. Crunching on an apple and relaxing.

It is difficult being confined. I am for the most part able to keep my mind free from the reality by staying busy. But when faced with some quiet time, I sometimes am forced to face the fact that my options are limited and that I am very alone. I miss simple things. I miss people. I miss gathering together in groups with a variety of faces to look at. I do not sulk about it, nor am I crushed under the weight of my circumstance. And while I do not continually think about my confinement and my restricted life in space, at times the thought comes to me: Wouldn't it be nice to be back living a normal life on the planet.

Good night John. I will be seeing you in a month or so (joy of joys!). In the meantime, I'll be watching over you.

Love,
Dad

27 April 1997
Letter B

Happy Russian Orthodox Easter

Dear John,

I just finished talking with Mommy on the radio. She tells me that I will hardly recognize you because you have gotten so big. That must mean that you have ceased to do your "spit the food out" trick. Great news!

I also talked with the Patriarch of the Russian Orthodox Church, Alexei II. His role in the church is similar to that of the Pope in the Roman Catholic Church. Today is the day that Easter is observed in Russia, and he wished the crew a blessed Easter and a safe journey, and Vasily and me good luck on our upcoming space walk.

Then he just sort of chatted, normal-like. He knew my name —asking how Jerry was doing. I told him that I was listening and that I was doing just great. He commented that he did not realize that I spoke Russian. Realizing that I did not know the Russian equivalent of "Your Excellency," I replied simply, *"Da, nemnoga"* ("Yes, a little"). I did not want to fib to the Patriarch. We then chatted a bit about life in space. He seemed fascinated. Afterward, I did a pretty good rendition of the resurrection as I floated away from the headset toward the ceiling.

We could not find any eggs to boil, but we did have a relaxing day. This was the first time since I have been up here that I actually took a day off work. I read a few short stories from a book entitled *Bad Trips*. Someone, I think a member of Shannon Lucid's family, had a good sense of humor when selecting that book to send to her when she was on the space station. The book contained stories of being stranded in airports, of trekking through deserts with water in short supply, and of flying through ice storms. The most miserable bad trip that I read about was one where the traveler was dry, comfortable, well fed, and not in imminent danger, but was stuck on a tour bus for an *entire day* with a boring guide. The guide, armed with a scratchy microphone with an overpoweringly loud speaker, talked the entire time about historical events and the dates that they occurred. That would be torture.

I understand that the space shuttle *Atlantis* was moved out to the launch pad today in Florida. Final preparations are underway. I talked to the STS-84 crew and they said that they completed their final integrated simulation. Integrated simulation means that instead of just practicing mission procedures and contingencies alone as a crew, people in both Mission Control–Moscow and Mission Control–Houston worked with the shuttle crew during real-time training. They practiced their responses to simulated emergencies and also performed a simulated docking of the shuttle to the *Mir*. The crew assured me that they were able to successfully dock in spite of the many malfunctions thrown at them during the exercise. I told them that I, too, was ready and that I would be standing by to open the door and join them after their arrival.

Happy Russian Orthodox Easter, John. I am passing along some of the blessings I received from the Patriarch to you and Mommy and adding a prayer of my own.

Good night. Sleep tight, my little guy. See you in a wink.

Love,
Dad

28 April 1997

Not to Worry

Dear John,
It is four-thirty in the afternoon, time for bed. I will get up at one-thirty in the morning in order to do final preparations for the spacewalk. I will open the door and together Vasily and I will leave the space station for about six hours, starting precisely at seven-fifty tomorrow morning.

This schedule reminds me of our time flips when traveling back and forth between Russia and the United States. Maybe that jet lag training will come in handy after all.

Sleep tight. I will hang on tight the whole time that I am outside of the space station, I promise.

Love you. A kiss for Mommy please. Tell her not to worry.

Dad

Back Home, Safe and Sound

Dear John,

Went walking. The fresh air that I breathed inside the space suit felt good.

Back home, safe and sound.

Good night to you. Love and miss you.

Dad

What Is a Space Walk Like?

Dear John,

Whenever someone has eaten some unusual meat, say rabbit, deer, dog, or frog, invariably the question "What did it taste like?" is asked. People usually say chicken, but know that it really did not taste just like chicken but rather exactly like rabbit, deer, dog, or frog.

Try this one yourself. What does beef taste like? Your reply? Pork? Bacon? Chicken? All answers are not quite right, are they? Beef tastes like beef, period.

What does a space walk feel like? Like a space walk. But let me give you the "sorta like chicken" answer, so that you at least have a feel for it.

It is important to remember that all space walks are different. A space walk performed over great distances on the surface of a sprawling space station has a different flavor from one conducted inside the confines of the cargo bay of the space shuttle. In turn, each of these space walks is a different experience from space walks conducted dangling outside of a capsule and attached to an umbilical cord, or one where the astronaut is rambling on the Moon's surface. When Mommy makes spicy chicken, I cannot even eat it. The same meat changes its flavor drastically depending on the recipe.

As far as how my space walk felt, imagine this. You are in scuba gear. Your vision is restricted by the size of your underwater mask. Your fins, wetsuit, and gloves make you clumsy and bulky. The water is frigid; in fact, it is thickly frozen overhead with only one entry-exit hole drilled into the ice. Your life depends on your gear functioning properly the entire time. The farther away you venture, the farther away you are from the reentry hole drilled in the ice. With increased distance from the hole, you become less tolerant of and more susceptible to any failure whatsoever.

There are no bottom, no sides, no top. Up and down are confused. The path from one point to another is not straight and unobstructed, but rather obstacle-filled and on a constantly convex, and thus falling away, primary surface. As you round one obstacle, the next appears. Soon enough it is difficult to determine your way back to the start.

You are not in water, but on a cliff. Crawling, slithering, gripping, reaching. You are not falling from the cliff; instead, the whole cliff is falling and you are on it. You convince yourself that it is okay for the cliff and yourself on the cliff to be falling because when you look down you see no bottom. You just *fall* and *fall* and *fall*.

The Sun sets swiftly. Blackness totally envelops you. The darkness in not merely dark, but absolute black. You see nothing, *nothing*. You squeeze the handhold ever more tightly. You convince yourself that it is okay to be falling, alone, nowhere, in the blackness. After a bit of self-doubt, you convince yourself that you are an astronaut and that you are trained to do this and that failure is not an option. You loosen your grip.

Your eyes finally adjust to the darkness and you can begin to make out forms. Another human, your space walking partner, is being silhouetted against the heavens. When it first became dark, you were falling feet first. Now, five minutes later, as the cliff—which is the space station itself— rotates, you feel as if you have reached the crest of the roller coaster and are now barreling down steeply. So steeply that you have the sensation of falling headfirst out of your seat and toward Earth. You now feel as if you are falling spread eagle, head first, toward Earth. You rationally know that you are still attached to the space station and that the station, not yourself, has rotated. But you *feel* differently, you *feel* upside-down. You want to flip back upright, but you cannot mentally make it happen. You finally convince yourself that it is okay to be diving headfirst into nothing.

You need to work with your hands. You must convince yourself to let go of the handrail and to trust that your tethers will hold. You depend on the two tethers that you had carefully placed on handholds to hold you securely in place. Once you let go and begin to work with both of your hands, you dangle. You rotate, twist, and float; all motion is random and uncontrolled. Still the cliff is falling and rotating. You know that you are falling with it, you tell yourself that surely you are falling with it because your tethers are attached. Yet it is difficult to discount the sensation that *you are moving away*, alone and detached.

Climbing out to the end of a telescoping rod that will be your means of moving to a different space station module, you feel as if you are at the end of an overmatched fishing pole. The pole keeps getting longer and longer and thinner and thinner as you are thrust out farther and farther. You feel the way a hooked fish must feel on the end of a flimsy rod. The pole sways back and forth, and you, being attached, sway back and forth. The pole no longer looks rigid and straight, but rather like a skinny S-curve. You are hanging to the thinnest limb of the tallest tree in the strongest wind. The tree is falling. You convince yourself that it is an oak, that the limb will stay attached and will not fracture, and that the forest bottom is far away.

In the midst of all of this chaos, you carry out your work calmly and methodically. You even snap a picture or two and notice that the Straits of Gibraltar, connecting the Atlantic to the Mediterranean, are passing by below you.

That is how it felt, the best that I can describe it. What was actually taking place?

I opened the door of the airlock and climbed out onto a horizontal ladder. With my partner following, we transferred a dresser-sized optical properties monitor (OPM) experiment along the convex surface of the space station module, past protruding, sharp-edged solar sensors, solar panels, and other equipment. Arriving at the end of a long telescoping transfer pole, we then attached the OPM and myself to the end of the pole.

My partner, using a three-foot diameter ring that encircled the pole, slid along the length of the pole—fifteen meters or so—to its base. The base was located on a different module of the space station. Once at the base of the pole, Vasily positioned himself to operate the hand crank mechanical controls that would allow him to swing and to extend the pole.

Vasily then swung the OPM and me away from the attachment point. The tip of the pole was telescoped out farther, and then translated toward a different module. This movement was done very precisely and with many midcourse corrections, which I called out to Vasily. We had to change the direction of movement often in order not to collide with solar panels. I eventually ended up at the distant end of a third, and even more distant, space station module.

Upon arrival, I fastened the tip of the pole to its new location. Vasily shimmied up the pole to rejoin me, and we worked together to install the OPM. A third cosmonaut, inside the space station, confirmed that our cable connections were good by running some diagnostic tests. We returned by the same means to the original module, where we detached and retrieved two large (1.5-meter-square) cosmic dust/space debris collector panels for return to Earth. We also attached a radiation dosimeter and then reentered the airlock with the experiment panels.

Closing the outer hatch, we then pressurized the airlock. After the pressure in the airlock was equalized to the pressure within the rest of the space station, we then opened the first inner hatch. At this point it was safe to get out of our spacesuits. The space station smelled like a gasoline station in comparison to the fresh air we had been breathing inside the space suits for the previous five hours. We then opened the second inner hatch and returned to our home, just in time for dinner.

After a hearty dinner, I did some required post-space-walk work in the airlock and then dove into bed. I slept soundly and contentedly; all of our tasks accomplished flawlessly. (These are the words of the ground controllers, and they will get no argument from me—everything was carried out as planned.)

Good night, John. I hope that you are not awakened by a nightmare where you are falling, falling. The space shuttle will be coming soon to pick me up. It is all down hill from here.

Love,
Dad

One Hundred Thirty-Two Days, Four Hours, One Minute

May was a busy month on board *Mir*. Having completed my space walk, it was time to turn my attention to packing up and getting ready to leave. For the first time in the mission, I let my guard down and started looking homeward once again. I would be leaving and could now begin to count the days, not the months, remaining.

I reviewed everything that had been accomplished and carved out time to complete any items left undone. I had sacrificed a lot. The reward would be in knowing that I had given it my best and that I had served my U.S. Navy, my country, and all the people of Earth well. I made sure that I had completed 100 percent of our mission goals. Remarkably, in spite of the numerous difficulties on board, all tasks were indeed complete.

I started thinking more about my family and our reunion. I worked out harder than ever on the treadmill and with bungee cords, trying to ready my body for the onslaught of gravity. Except for the longer hair and scruffy face, when I looked in the mirror I did not notice anything much different about my appearance. I began to daydream about the things that I wanted to do back on the planet.

Eventually, I had to pack up the hard drive of the computer I was using to type my letters to John. When the shuttle arrived, I was able to send my final letter to him over *Atlantis's* communication system. The joyous thought that *I am going home* was never far from my consciousness during my last few weeks aboard the space station *Mir*.

When I landed, I had spent one hundred thirty-two days, four hours, and one minute of continuous time in space. Near the end, even the *minutes* began to count.

Made It to May

Dear John,

Hooray! I made it to May.

May 1st remains a Russian holiday. During the Soviet period, it was May Day. Since the fall of Communism, the Russians, reluctant to give up a holiday, have been trying to figure out just what they are celebrating on that particular day. Although Sunday is normally our designated rest day up here, I noticed that my schedule for Sunday is booked solid with work. To be honest, regardless of what is on the schedule, Sunday has never been a day of rest. Instead, we use it, rather futilely I might add, to try to catch up on all the work not yet completed during the week.

Mommy and I always got a kick out of the Russian holiday system when we were together in Star City. If the holiday falls on, say, a Thursday, we would have that Thursday off. But then when we would look at the upcoming training schedule, we would notice that a full day of training was planned for Saturday. When we would ask why we had to work on Saturday, the response, always accompanied with a look that said, "Why do you ask such an obvious question?" was "To make up for the time that you missed on Thursday."

Two-day holidays completely wipe out your upcoming weekend and can set you up for a stretch of ten workdays without a break. After realizing that every "holiday" comes complete with an accompanying payback day, we began to prefer months like March over December because there were fewer holidays in March!

I hope that my letter yesterday did not cause you any nightmares of falling last night. Speaking of sleep, starting tonight and for the next twelve days, I will begin my final interval of sleep studies. The setup includes eye monitors, electrodes, thermometer to record body temperature, blood, surveys, and dream recall recordings—the whole shebang. I will let you know if I dream that I am falling off a cliff, okay?

To put your mind at ease, the sensation of falling during the space walk was okay. It just took some getting used to. Interestingly, I never felt that sensation when I was inside either the space station or the shuttle. I think that part of the sensation, the flipping part, was probably due to the orientation of the space station relative to Earth, which slowly changed as the space walk progressed.

Sweet, peaceful dreams. If all goes as planned, I will be seeing you before the end of the month. Great joy!

Love,
Dad

2 May 1997

My Orlan M Spacewalking Suit

Dear John,

I have a great picture of you hanging on the bulkhead. You are dressed in overalls and looking at the ground inquisitively, as if you had just spotted your first grasshopper and are unsure whether to touch it or to run. You don't look like a baby, but rather like a little man, perhaps a farmer, in those overalls.

Maybe you caught a glimpse of me in my space suit the other day and thought, "Boy, is Dad ever dressing strangely these days. I should lend him a pair of my overalls." Let me tell you about my Orlan M spacewalking suit and maybe you will understand why overalls just would not do.

The Orlan M space suit is the latest fashion, a brand new model, never used in space before yesterday. The people at the Zvesda ("star" in Russian) company in Moscow designed the suit. They also built the first spacewalking suit ever used by the Russians back in the sixties.

The suit comes in one color, off-white, and weighs about one hundred and seventy-five pounds. I climbed into the suit through a "back door." I could close the door myself by pulling a wire that is attached to the door and winds its way around the exterior of the left side of the space suit to the front. By grabbing a fastening ring located on the very end of the wire and then hooking it over an attachment point on the chest area of the suit I can keep the door loosely closed.

The door is snugged up airtight and locked shut by pulling up on a metal lever on the right hip section. While all of this rigging is rather complex, the advantage is that, unlike you, John, theoretically I can get dressed by myself. In actuality, Vasily and I helped each other don our suits. It is better to have someone behind you to ensure that nothing is caught in the sealing ring when one closes the door.

The suit is cramped inside. Because I had grown two inches since being in space, my head struck the top of the space suit. Hunched over, I felt like a sardine in a can.

Once the door is closed, the suit needs to start providing air, carbon dioxide scrubbing, moisture removal (to prevent fogging of the visor), and cooling. The suit comes equipped with two oxygen tanks, a primary and a reserve. The reserve is used only if the primary tank malfunctions or becomes exhausted. The carbon dioxide scrubber consists of a bed of chemicals that absorb and bind this exhaled metabolic waste product. The moisture is gathered into a wick-like material. The air within the suit is circulated using a series of fans, ducting, and shunts.

Chilled water that circulates through tubes sewn into an inner garment provides cooling. The circulating water carries away the metabolic heat that is produced as we work. Inlet and outlet fittings from the inner garment tubes are mated to the pressure suit itself. Two pumps, a primary pump and a backup pump, circulate the water. The fluid passes through a heat exchanger, which in turn is cooled by evaporating (actually, sublimating) water over a series of baffles into the vacuum of space.

Electrical power for the suit is supplied by battery and a radio is used for communications. We also used the radio to pipe in some music from the space station whenever we found ourselves in darkness and waiting for sunrise in order to resume working once again. These rest intervals occurred every hour or so and lasted about twenty minutes each. We would be in complete darkness, listening to rock and roll music, whizzing through space. Pretty wild. Finally, we were hooked up to EKG and body temperature sensor probes, which sent their signals directly to the ground via telemetry.

Suit pressure gauges, oxygen pressure gauges, control panels, and a caution and warning panel are all located on the upper chest area of the suit. Because of this convenient location, I was able to periodically look down through my visor and monitor all the critical suit parameters. I kept a close watch on the gauges throughout the space walk. I did hear one master alarm during the space walk. Hearing the alarm, I immediately scanned suit pressure and oxygen level, the two most critical elements for survival, and was relieved to see that both were normal. It turned out that the alarm was actually originating from inside the space station and we heard it via the radio. Although the problem was a minor one and did not immediately concern us, it did take a few minutes before my pulse returned to normal! The emergency indicators on the space suit remained quiet and unlit the entire space walk.

Those are the components that make up the Orlan M space suit. The suit is an amazing piece of gear—essentially an independent spacecraft that allowed me to work on the exterior of the space station while being protected from the harsh, life-threatening environment of space.

I still like your coveralls, John. Good night. Be good, but adventurous. A little naughty is okay.

Love,
Dad

PS: Grasshoppers won't bite. Chase 'em next time.

Lost in Space

Dear John,

One of these days you will get lost.

Maybe you will be shopping with Mommy at the grocery store or with me at the hardware store and suddenly you will realize that you do not see anyone familiar. Although we might be located only one aisle away or on the other side of a counter, fear will set in. From your vantage—eye level at about two feet—a meat counter might as well be a mountain.

The space station sprawls. Modules go out in all directions. On the surface of each module protrude solar panels, sun sensors, tanks, experiments, telescope mounts, and various "bumps" that accommodate equipment that would not quite fit inside the confines of the cylindrical walls of the station.

The flat-surfaced solar panels stick out perpendicular to the axis of the modules. They look like enormous wings coming off the station, continually rotating in order to keep as much of their energy-gathering surfaces facing the Sun. The panels are located on all six modules; module *Spektr* alone has six solar panels protruding.

Because of all the clutter, during the space walk we were, for the most part, lost.

Not lost lost. Not "in the middle of the woods hearing bears growl" lost, but more like your possible experience of being "behind the meat counter" lost. I would say that for the majority of our time spacewalking we were unsure of our exact location. Amidst the clutter, it was at times hard to determine which way was up or what was on the other side of the bump next to us. Most of the time I was unsure which direction we had come from just two minutes prior.

For the most part, my face was no farther than two feet from the surface that I was moving along. I was dragging along a desk-size experiment. I could not get far enough away from the surface of *Mir* to see the "big picture" unless I let go of the handrail completely and floated away, constrained only by my tethers. In general, letting go is not the thing to do, since that action increases my chance of becoming forever detached from the station. Furthermore, unlike the situation inside the shuttle payload bay, where the spacewalker is somewhat cradled by the concave surface, the surface of the *Mir* space station is always convex, always moving away, always dropping off from view. The convex shape of the space station modules might be part of the reason why one feels the "falling off" sensation some of the time when working on the exterior of the space station.

With a bulging bump to the right, a solar panel below, and a star sensor above, one's field of view becomes rapidly diminished. At times, even the handrail ahead was blocked by an attached experiment. I would be forced to backtrack and then travel down a new route in order to get to my destination. Furthermore, the space suit visor, though adequately shaped, inherently restricted my field of view still more. When all of these factors are combined, moving from point A to point B was difficult at best.

The various obstructions and the difficulties they pose to movement from one place to another are part of the reason why the space station is equipped with two telescoping booms. The booms allow an attached spacewalker to be swung through the open spaces between modules to distant modules, thereby avoiding the necessity of crawling over the cluttered surfaces of the station. But when one is trying to swing the boom through the free space between modules, the outstretched solar panels become an obstruction. On numerous occasions the boom and I—dangling on the end of the boom—were within inches of the delicate, sharp-edged solar panels.

When I was attached to the tip of the boom and swung out away from the module, my perspective improved drastically. I was now far enough away from the surface of the space station to see the different parts of *Mir* with an unobstructed view. As we kept increasing the length of the pole by telescoping it out, I got farther and farther away and the station became smaller and smaller, to the point where I began to get downright lonely out there by myself!

Oh, I should tell you this little story. After quite a struggle in trying to get to and then retrieve an experiment (termed MSRE) that had been attached to the station, we were finally successful. I handed Vasily the MSRE panel and he tucked it under his arm. This task accomplished, Vasily and I decided that I would head off to find and then detach the PIE panel (a different experiment), while he would begin returning some of the items already gathered to the airlock. We both pushed off, floating free from the handrail, in order to get our bearings and figure out the direction to the airlock. But because of all the clutter, we could not gain a view of the big picture, which we needed in order to become oriented.

After a minute or so of fruitless bobbing, I spotted a port-hole. I floated up to it and looked through the window to the *inside* of the space station. By looking inside, I was able to see familiar landmarks and thus gain the needed perspective. Fully oriented and pointing, I told Vasily, "The airlock is that way; the PIE panel, that way. I'll see you back there when I finish." Only by looking *inside* the station were we able to become oriented to our position on the *outside* of the station.

Sleep soundly. Don't go walking in your sleep (and get lost!).

Love you and miss you.

Dad

4 May 1997

Packing Up and Letting Go

Dear John,

I sure have been blabbing a lot lately, haven't I? I think that maybe I have gotten my second (or third or fourth!) wind now that I can see the end of the tunnel.

Welcome to America, welcome home! While you probably spent the day unpacking, I spent the day packing.

Packing up here is pretty much like packing for a move back on the planet. Everything is listed on an inventory list. Finding the items is the first challenge, and then finding a place to put the packed bag the second challenge. On the positive side of space packing, there is no piano to move; in fact, nothing is heavy. My back is never sore at the end of the day from lifting too much. On the negative side, I cannot simply place items into a bag. Instead, I have to open the lid partially, stuff the item inside, and then close the bag quickly before all the other items already inside the bag float away.

The chief of the astronaut office wrote me a short note of apology the other day. He informed me that he was going to his son's wedding and will not, therefore, be down at Cape Canaveral to greet me when I land. He said that he remembers distinctly his son crawling around in their backyard, trying to keep his knees off the ground in order to avoid the pricks of fallen pine needles, a lot of years ago. His son is now a graduate of the U.S. Naval Academy, an officer in the U.S. Marines, and is about to be married.

It must feel good to know that you have succeeded as a parent, that your son or daughter "turned out" okay, and that they are out on their own and doing well.

It must hurt to let go. To realize that your children, now young adults, really do not need you as they once did. It must hurt to know that you will not be seeing them quite as often as before and that the sight of them crawling around gingerly among pine needles will no longer warm your heart.

Good night, John. Please pass along one of your sweetest of kisses to Mommy for me. Miss you both.

Dad

Higher Than Michael Jordan

Hello John,

The more I pack things up, the more I am certain that you would really, really enjoy playing hide-and-seek up here. I almost got my whole body behind some panels today trying to retrieve items.

I can also play a mean air guitar, jump higher than Michael Jordan, and win a gold medal in gymnastics up here. Although I will undoubtedly miss some of these when I return to Earth, I am looking forward to rediscovering all that the planet has to offer.

Take green grass in the summer. What a color! Green. Green, green, green. Ah, so soothing to lie in. So soft and cool in the shade. Being carefree and picking three-leaf clover or perhaps getting lucky and finding a four-leafer. Green nice-on-your-eyes green. Throw in a buzzing bumblebee and a butterfly or two for action and you cannot ask for more, can you?

On Earth, one does not have to make the air; it is just *there* for the breathing. If the toilet breaks, there are plenty of trees. The doors open to *something*. Birds chirp and life surrounds in abundance. Water is drawn from lakes and rivers. One can eat hot apple pie topped with frozen ice cream.

I do not know what life is like for other living beings in the universe, but we got lucky being born Earthlings. Leave and one quickly comes to appreciate the wonders all the more.

Tonight, I will be sleeping with something—electrodes and eye sensors. And before crawling into bed, Dracula will visit me and take more of my blood. I would rather sleep alone, or better yet, with Mommy. Soon enough.

Good night. I was going to tell you to cuddle up with your blankie or teddy bear, but you never did much go for that, did you, John? You prefer the thumb. Pleasant dreams. Miss you. A kiss for Mommy please.

Love,
Dad

6 May 1997

Your Dad Has Courage

Dear John,

Courage is a hard thing to define. The same action that can be called courageous for one person might not be for another, depending on their prior experience.

For example, diving into a lake to save a drowning person is an act of extreme courage for someone who does not know how to swim. Yet, for an Olympic gold-medal swimmer like Mark Spitz, the act would be no big deal.

Circumstances can change the equation. Picture this: icy seas and big waves, on board a ship plying the North Atlantic. Someone falls overboard. Strong swimmer or not, if someone dives in and attempts a rescue, it is a courageous act once again.

Timing matters, also. If the event happens so fast that the rescuer merely acted on instinct, it somehow lessens the degree of courage exhibited. An example might be someone diving in for the save but without considering, a priori, that the waters are shark-infested.

Finally, the background of the person doing the evaluating matters a lot. If the rescuer did something that would be frightening to the observer, the act subjectively seems all the more courageous.

Astronauts and cosmonauts launch into space in rockets. Rockets have awesome power. Launching them entails big risks—one cannot argue with that. To most observers, the people inside are brave souls.

But when climbing into a rocket, I cannot say that I ever felt particularly courageous or brave. I just did it, primarily because that was what I was prepared to do, that was what I had been trained to do. Butterflies flew higher when I was on deck in the bottom of the ninth in a tight game playing Little League baseball.

Coming to live on a space station? In my mind, I saw it as a great adventure and an opportunity to explore. More or less, the culmination of why I had chosen to become an astronaut in the first place. I had some trepidation, yes; but not so much as to make me reach deep and summon all the courage that I could muster before setting off.

The space station *Mir* has had its problems during my stay on board. The summary list of problems I saw written in the newspapers (the article relayed to me via telemetry) included fire; loss of attitude control and tumbling through space; breakdown of two oxygen-generating systems; breakdown of the carbon dioxide absorbing system; and leaks in the cooling system pipes, contaminating the atmosphere with ethylene glycol and causing the temperature to soar to over ninety-five degrees inside. (They missed our intermittent toilet problems, the problem that most concerned us, the crew!)

Let's look at each of these events. The fire? I reacted on instinct, on a sense of survival. Tumbling? It was a gentle tumble, not like doing barrel rolls or loops in a Navy jet. System problems? They were more nagging, since they were not so acutely life threatening. Some tough times, yes, but we would methodically work through the problems, overcome them, and then redouble our efforts. Heat? Since we astronauts train in Houston, the weeks-long ninety-five degree temperature merely reminded me of home. Now, as for my Russian cosmonaut crewmates, the high heat took some getting used to!

Do not get me wrong, these have been tough times. But having gone through all of this, I cannot say that I ever truly felt courageous.

I am too tired to write much more tonight, John, and this letter is already too long. But I want you to know that your *Dad has courage*. Without getting into details, I can tell you that during the space walk I needed courage—raw courage—to get the job done. I felt courage distinctly, clearly, and just the uncomfortable way I always thought that courage would feel. I compartmentalized my fear and pressed on in order to complete the mission. And let me tell you another thing that I learned about true courage: When the brave act is over, one does not feel boastful about the accomplishment, nor is one excited by it. In fact, I did not even want to think about it, let alone talk about it for a few days thereafter. After courage is spent, the only thing that one feels is relief.

I am also relieved that you are home, safe and sound. Mommy's voice sounded so good to me today when I talked to her on the ham radio. I can't wait for us to get back together again. Sleep tight.

Love,
Dad

Baby Feet

Dear John,

The soles of my feet are now as soft as yours are.

Calluses soften the first month, hang in there the second month, peel off a bit the third month and flake off profusely the fourth month. From there on out I have had baby feet. I would bet that you never even thought about things like that, and probably wish that I had not told you about them either!

My neck veins continue to be engorged. The condition reminds me of patients that I used to treat who suffered from congestive heart failure. But the puffiness in the face, which most astronauts experience as body fluids shift toward the head in weightlessness and which I got only a mild case of, has disappeared long ago. I think you will still be able to recognize me.

Fingernails seem to grow faster, toenails more slowly, and hair longer. The hair grows longer not only on the top of my head, but also on my arms and legs.

Without gravity pulling down on my body, I am close to two inches taller than when I left. I am just trying to keep up with your rate of growth, John. But I will shrink back down to normal when I arrive back on the planet, so you will win the "who grew the most in five months" contest. While back pain is not uncommon in cosmonauts and astronauts as they "grow" in space, my back continues to feel fine.

My digestive system has not changed noticeably. I still eat enough for two people and am hungry as a permanent state of being.

Strength-wise, while I do not feel weaker, I know that I am. I have not been truly challenged physiologically in a long time. Every so often Mission Control–Moscow monitors my exercise sessions on the treadmill and bicycle. In fact, I just completed my final three-day set of these one hour each, twice daily sessions.

Instead of doing the required routine, I pretty much doubled or tripled what the ground expects of me. Throughout my stay on *Mir*, I have been running at faster rates and, when time permits, doubling the prescribed duration of time on the treadmill. I have been using two expanders—bungee cord–like devices used to maintain strength—instead of one when doing squats. Given my dedication to staying in shape, I can at least claim that I am in no worse shape than the other cosmonauts who have been up here for long periods of time. We will see how I hold up after landing. Hiking with you riding piggyback will be my strength test.

Sleep seemed normal the first two months; but now it seems like the alarm goes off way too early each morning. During the day, I often feel like napping. Mommy and I might be more compatible in this department now than we were previously. This is not good, however, considering that we have another baby on the way! With you still wanting occasional nighttime and full-time daytime attention, and with a new baby needing middle-of-the-night feedings and changings, Mommy and I will *really* have our hands full.

While there have been plenty of things to be anxious about up here, I remain calm, worry-free, and generally content and happy. Just my nature, I suppose. Don't worry, be happy.

I hope that you, too, are feeling 100 percent well, John. Have a good night's sleep. I am looking forward to tucking you in once again when I get home. Getting up for you in the middle of the night won't be so bad either. Pleasant dreams. I miss you.

Love,
Dad

10 May 1997

A Bit Lonely for Mommy

Dear John,

It is "moving back in" day for you today. Now that I think about it, this will be the first time in your eighteen months of life that you will live in our house in Texas. Mommy said that she wants everything in order for when I return and for when the new baby arrives.

I suppose that you spent the day exploring the place. You probably already have discovered that you can make a loop from living room through entryway and back into the living room. I can just picture you: wide-eyed and with that look of "how did I end up here again" on your face, before tearing around the corner to try the loop again.

Maybe you found the big bed . . . I mean . . . your big trampoline. I hope that you like your room, although, for your first few nights, I bet that Mommy will keep you close by her. Safe, sound, and feeling secure.

The TV is scrawny and tucked away upstairs. That is the way we prefer it, little used. Be careful on the balcony and remind Mommy to do a head check, making sure you cannot fit between the slats and fall.

Perhaps it is lonely for Mommy, back in our home but without me there. You will have to fill in for me, John, for just a bit longer. Good night. Sleep tight. You are finally home, sweet home.

Love,
Dad

11 May 1997

Mother's Day

Dear John,

Don't forget that today is Mother's Day. I will help you write your Mother's Day letter. Attached is a copy of a note that you can give to Mommy, accompanied by one of your kisses, of course.

John's Mother's Day Letter

Dear Mommy,

I am the luckiest little hooligan in the world to have you as my mommy.

You are the funnest person to play with. When I put the cylinder-shaped block into the round hole, you clap. When I put the star-shaped block into the star-shaped hole, I draw more applause. I go on and on while you keep dumping the blocks out again and again. I start over again, you dump again. To be honest, I don't know why you like playing with the blocks so much. But since you seem so happy doing it and I aim to please, I keep putting the blocks back into the same holes until I just can't stand the boredom any longer!

You are my bestest pal. We hang around together all of the time. When we travel on airplanes together, you either chase me up and down the aisles or let me spill the food tray onto your lap. I especially like it when, after ten hours of being wide awake on the airplane, the minute I hear the landing gear come down I fall asleep like a rock. This, of course, gets your attention because you are worried that my ears will not clear and that I will be deaf for the rest of my life.

It is also great fun when you want to give me medicine. This game I especially enjoy. I perform the moving-target trick, turning my head back and forth and side to side with as much vigor as I can muster. It is fun to watch you trying to distract me by giving me the egg timer, the spoon, or the nesting doll. If the medicine tastes good, I will sometimes play along with you and allow you to sneak in one or two spoonfuls. But by now I know all of your tricks, and if the medicine tastes bad, you might as well give up.

You are with me day and night. I can depend on you. I know that you will take care of me and will love me no matter what I do.

At the end of the day, when I am sitting on your lap with you reading me my bedtime story, I feel oh so lucky. You make me feel special, as if I am the only thing in the whole wide world that matters to you and that you would do anything for me. And when you tuck me in, safe and sound, I feel safe and sound. My eyes get heavy. I feel the blanket coming up toward my neck and then I feel your tender kiss. The last thought that I have is, "Boy, am I a lucky little hooligan to have Mommy."

I love you Mommy. Happy Mother's Day. I cannot wait until you show me that baby that you have been hiding in your tummy.

John

Nice job, John. Good night. I'll be watching over you both. Send along my love to Mommy also, and tell her that I agree with you. We are both lucky hooligans to have her in our lives.

Dad

200

Ordering My First Earth Meal

Hello, Kathryn,

Thanks for your notes. As always, it was great to hear from you. It sounds like you have been quite popular on the TV circuit. You need to talk to Tom Brokow in person so that you can check him out, right (yuck, yuck)?

I am now sleeping on the shuttle. Good to be heading home.

In answer to your question, for my first Earth meal I would like to order your homemade meatloaf, mashed potatoes, and a *big, fresh* salad. Apple pie for dessert. To be honest, anything would be fine, even John's baby food leftovers, as long as it doesn't come in a tube!

John going to bed at seven o'clock in the evening is almost miraculous! Definitely keep him on that schedule! Wow. He finally is sleeping through the night, just in time for the next baby to sleep-deprive us!

I am glad to hear of everyone coming to Florida for my landing. I looked out of the window and the weather looked great down there today.

Love you. Can't wait to be together again.

Jerry

Aboard Atlantis—Standing Tall

Dear John,

I have changed post offices. This letter is being sent down from the space shuttle *Atlantis*, and in a day or so I will be home.

We closed the hatch last night between the *Mir* space station and the shuttle in order to be prepared for our early-morning departure. Following a gentle push-off, we began intermittently firing our thrusters. The bursts made loud bang-bang-bang sounds, similar in abruptness to cannon firing. As we moved away, the *Mir* became smaller, then smaller still. Finally, it was so diminished in size that the space station appeared to be nothing more that a rather insignificant blinking light among the stars.

Surprisingly, I felt very little emotion when leaving my home of the last one hundred and twenty-two days behind. I suppose that I just felt like my time was up, that I had done my duty, and that it was time for me to go. This is in stark contrast to the very strong emotion that I felt upon first seeing the space shuttle *Atlantis* arrive a few days ago. When I saw *Atlantis* approaching the *Mir*, I felt pure elation, pure unbridled joy.

I have an image in my mind of the time you took your first steps. I would move two steps away from you, leaving you standing and holding on, precariously, to the edge of the sofa. You would look at me with questioning eyes. Your eyes reflected what I am sure that you were asking yourself: "Can I do this, or will I fall?" After I would encourage you with a reassuring word or gesture, you would muster up your courage, let go, and walk to me.

Reporters keep asking me whether, after landing, I plan to get out of *Atlantis* on my own power or be carried off. I will be trying my best to follow in your footsteps, John. I will be giving it everything that I have to walk, or crawl, or do whatever it takes, but to do it on my own, just like you did.

I hope to be standing and holding you in a day or two, John.

Love,
Dad

Epilogue

I landed on May 24, 1997, after having spent a total of one hundred thirty-two days, four hours, and one minute in space. I had traveled roughly fifty million miles—the equivalent of going to the Moon and back one hundred ten times. I had circled Earth two thousand times. I had flown at speeds approaching 18,000 miles per hour on board the U.S. space shuttle *Atlantis*, the Russian *Soyuz*, and the Russian space station *Mir*. In addition, I flew alone outside the confines of any spacecraft whatsoever, spacewalking more than three orbits around the planet. And of importance to me personally, I finished what I started. Faced with immense difficulties and life-threatening occurrences on *Mir*, I took it to the end without giving up.

The last thing that I wanted my wife Kathryn to endure was seeing me being carried off *Atlantis* on a stretcher. That was the recommended option. I would have no part of it. I had overcome. I had endured. I was coming home the victor, not a defeated soul. After landing and gathering every ounce of strength that I could muster, I got out of my parachute, swung my legs to the side of the seat, stood, and walked. Oh, sure, it felt as if I had someone standing on my shoulders and I was doing back flips every time I turned my head ever so slightly, but so be it. I stood up and walked off, head held high. In my mind, I was representing the people of Earth. I wanted them all to realize and to take pride in the fact that the human spirit can overcome great obstacles and rise to the occasion time and time again.

Kathryn, less than a month away from delivering our second son, stood with John in her arms in the middle of a sterile-looking room. She looked beautiful. We embraced. John looked on with curiosity. He appeared to be relatively comfortable with me, a vaguely familiar man with long hair and a swaying stance, hugging his mommy. Kathryn began sobbing, overcome with emotion. John grew immediately defensive of his crying mother and turned from me to give her a comforting hug.

John looked huge. And when he became comfortable with me once again, I picked him up for a long-overdue hug. He felt heavy! Afraid that I might forget about the presence of Earth's gravity and drop him, I handed him back to his mommy. We shuffled away together as a family.

Kathryn eventually made the meatloaf, mashed potatoes, and fresh salad that I had requested from space as my "welcome home" meal. I spent a good deal of time in my backyard just looking at the grass, listening to birds, and appreciating, perhaps for the first time in my life, the fresh air and breeze in my face. I will no longer take the simple things of Earth for granted.

John and I have grown to be great pals once again. He is beautiful, fun-loving, and smart. He seems to enjoy his role as big brother to Jeffrey. After months of rehabilitation, my strength has returned. I can now pick John up with ease, give him horsey-back rides, and take him fishing. He likes the worms more than the fish. What a joy he is to me.

There is nothing in the universe as fantastic as your own flesh and blood. Nothing. We parents, mothers and fathers, should never forget this fact.

Good night my sons. I will always and forever be watching over you.

Dad

Index

211

About the Author

Jerry M. Linenger, M.D., Ph.D., at the completion of his mission to *Mir*, had spent more continuous time in space than any other male American astronaut. A Naval Academy graduate and physician, he holds advanced degrees from the University of North Carolina, the University of Southern California, and Wayne State University. The author of the best-selling memoir *Off the Planet: Five Perilous Months Aboard the Space Station Mir*, Linenger lives in Michigan with his wife, Kathryn, and their four young children.